Cowboys
OF THE
Sky

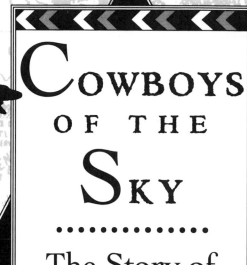

Cowboys
OF THE
Sky

· · · · · · · · · · · · ·

The Story of Alaska's Bush Pilots

· · · · · · · · · · · · ·

Steven C. Levi

Walker and Company
New York

First published in the United States of America in 1996 by Walker
Publishing Company, Inc.

Published simultaneously in Canada by Thomas Allen & Son Canada,
Limited, Markham, Ontario

Library of Congress Cataloging-in-Publication Data
Levi, Steven C.
Cowboys of the sky : the story of Alaska's bush pilots / Steven C. Levi.
    p.   cm.
Includes bibliographical references.
ISBN 0-8027-8331-7 (hardcover).—ISBN 0-8027-8332-5 (reinforced)
    1. Bush flying—Alaska—History.   2. Air pilots—Alaska—
Anecdotes.   3. Alaska—Description and travel.   I. Title.
    TL522.A4L48   1996
    629.13'092'2798—dc20   95-35284
                CIP

Photograph on title page appears courtesy of the Anchorage Museum of
History and Fine Art.

BOOK DESIGN BY CAROL MALCOLM RUSSO/SIGNET M. DESIGN, INC.

Printed in the United States of America

2   4   6   8   10   9   7   5   3   1

FOR
TATE CHANNING LONE

There are old pilots and bold pilots, but there
are no old, bold pilots.

—OLD ALASKA BUSH PILOT ADAGE

CONTENTS

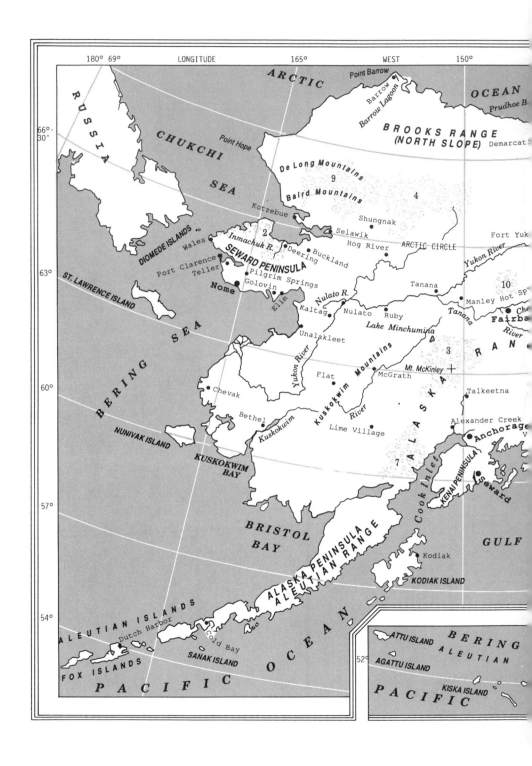

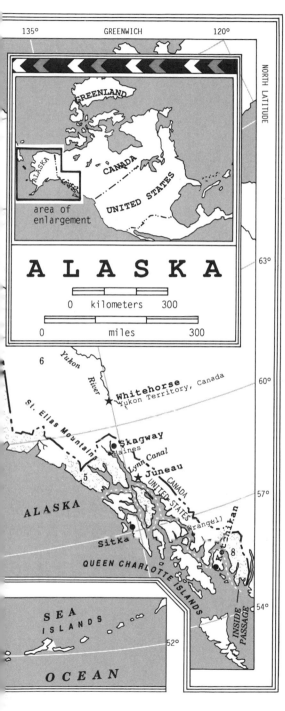

Cowboys
OF THE
Sky

1

Alaska and the Bush Plane

IN THE 1920s, DURING THE EARLY DAYS OF THE ALASKA
bush pilots, it was said that there were three types of weather. The
first was "Pan American weather." This was because Pan American
Airlines was famous for only flying when the sky was as clear as
glass. Then there was "flying weather," which varied depending on
which bush pilot was doing the talking. Finally, there was "Gillam
weather," when flying conditions were so bad that only Harold
"Thrill 'Em, Chill 'Em, Spill 'Em, But No Kill 'Em" Gillam would
fly. The modern term for such weather is "socked in," meaning that
dense fog covers the runway, threatening clouds form a dense ceiling
across the sky, and there are violent winds strong enough to jerk a
plane out of the sky.

Whenever there was Gillam weather, seasoned Alaska bush pilots
would sit out the bad spell, primarily because it was too dangerous to
fly and, secondarily, because, in their words, "God's plenty busy taking care of Harold."[1]

It wasn't that Gillam loved bad weather. It was just that he had no
objection to flying in thick soup. He had the eyes of a cat and did not

find it difficult to navigate with little or no visibility. As an example of his ability, in the midst of one particularly brutal night in the late 1930s, a number of Gillam's friends were grounded in McGrath. A storm was blasting with such intensity that, as Oscar Winchell, one of the grounded bush pilots, reported, "I wouldn't have whipped a cat out there that night." The pilots were sitting around a fire in a cabin when they heard a plane land. A bit later Gillam walked in, said hello to his friends, fueled his plane, and took off. Three days later those same bush pilots were still in McGrath waiting for the storm to lift, and Gillam was back in Fairbanks after having safely delivered his mail and supplies.

Gillam was the stuff from which legends are made. But then, so were Alaska's bush pilots, the cowboys of the sky.

*H*AROLD *G*ILLAM'S *F*AIRCHILD *P*ILGRIM AT *M*C*G*RATH ON A MAIL RUN. (*P*HOTOGRAPH COURTESY OF *J*IM *R*UOTSALA)

"God may have created Alaska," humorist Warren Sitka noted, "but it was the airplane that truly carved the face of the Last Frontier." Few Alaskans would argue with this statement. Seventy years ago—and last year—Alaska's bush pilots carried the groceries, delivered the mail, transported emergency medical personnel, and village-hopped an airborne Santa Claus from Demarcation Point to Unalakleet. Even in an age when Americans have walked on the moon, for villages like Wales, Alexander Creek, or Lake Minchumina, mail still only comes once a week—and that's during the summer.

Alaska is different from the forty-eight contiguous states, called the Lower 48 by Alaskans. More than a third of Alaska's people live in the bush, the 90 percent of the state that is unreachable by road. For these Alaskans, traveling a hundred miles is quite different than for anyone else in the United States. In the Lower 48, a trip of a hundred miles can be viewed as a little less than two hours by car. The average American climbs into an automobile and then pulls onto a highway or freeway. At sixty miles per hour the driver can leisurely eat up the hundred miles of blacktop in about an hour and forty minutes.

In Alaska, traveling a hundred miles can be like stepping back in time. First, even though Alaska is one-fifth the size of the Lower 48, there are less than 6,000 miles of paved road—less than in a medium-sized city like Riverside, California; El Paso, Texas; or Greensboro, North Carolina. A hundred-mile trip in Alaska will take significantly longer than one hour and forty minutes—even if the weather is good.

For residents of all bush communities, everything from toothpicks to prescription drugs must come in by barge or airplane. Barges are efficient when it comes to moving cargo in tons, but few villages buy many supplies by the ton. And the yearly barge can arrive only during the 120 days a year when the Bering Sea and the rivers are ice-free.

Even with the bush plane, Alaskan communities remain isolated. Historically, this is not unusual. The first Siberians who walked across the Bering Sea land bridge 15,000 years ago arrived in an area in which they had no choice but to live in small communities. They lived off the land, much as their descendants do today.

When the Russian fur traders arrived in the mid-1700s, they struggled with the same problems that plague bush Alaskans today. During the summer mosquitoes, gnats, and biting flies swarmed in clouds, and the swampy tundra made overland transportation impossible. Ice covered the Bering Sea eight months a year. When snow shrouded the land and the insects were in hibernation, inland travel was easier, but the low temperatures and long distances between settlements made any journey treacherous.

At first, trading for furs proved to be beneficial for both the Russians and the Natives. The Russians got the furs they wanted and the Natives received products they could not make, such as steel knives. Soon there was a flourishing trade between the two parties. But the profitable years for the Russian–American Company did not last: The company went bankrupt. In 1867 the United States bought Alaska for $7.2 million. Though the purchase made the United States the owner of Alaska, the presence of the federal government was barely felt in the new territory. There were a handful of military governors and scattered pockets of American soldiers. The fur trade continued and, offshore, American whalers plied the waters of the Bering Sea and Arctic Ocean in search of the bowhead whale. For the most part Alaskans were left to fend for themselves.

That all changed with the discovery of gold just before the turn of the century. Alaska's two major strikes at Nome and Fairbanks drew 100,000 men and 10,000 women to the northland. The Alaska gold rush was unique for two reasons. First, it affected all parts of the territory, from Barrow on the shores of the Arctic Ocean in the north to Ketchikan in the rain forest of southeastern Alaska and Dutch Harbor in the Aleutians. Second, it was one of the longest gold rushes in world history. It began with the discovery of gold in what is now Juneau in the 1880s and lasted until the mines shut down during the Second World War.

One of the most important results of the gold rush was the sudden increase in the population; hundreds of small bush communities sprang to life because of the gold industry. When the town of Nome exploded from a handful of men to a full-fledged city of 20,000 resi-

AN *AUTHENTIC ALASKA GOLD RUSH CLAIM ON THE IMNUCHUK RIVER, NEAR KOTZEBUE, IN SEP-TEMBER 1903. THE ACTUAL MINE IS BELOW THE BARREL ON THE WINCH IN THE CENTER OF THE PHOTOGRAPH. BECAUSE THE GROUND IS FROZEN, THE SOIL IN THE MINE HAS TO BE THAWED. WATER IS TURNED TO STEAM IN THE BOILER ON THE RIGHT AND THEN PIPED INTO THE MINE UNDER PRESSURE. (NOTE THE STEAM LINE RUNNING FROM THE BOILER TO THE MINE.) WHEN THE EARTH AT THE BOTTOM OF THE PIT HAS BEEN THAWED, IT IS PLACED IN THE BARREL AND PULLED UP OUT OF THE MINE. THE EARTH IS THEN PILED OUTSIDE THE MINE—AS CAN BE SEEN ON THE LEFT SIDE OF THE PHOTOGRAPH—UNTIL IT CAN BE WASHED WITH WATER TO SEPARATE THE GOLD FROM THE OVERBURDEN. (PHOTOGRAPH BY NOWELL COURTESY OF THE UNIVERSITY OF WASHINGTON, NEG. 143)*

dents, it was suddenly economically feasible to ship cargo by the bargeload. As the gold rush extended up the Yukon and Kuskokwim rivers and their tributaries, it became profitable to barge supplies upriver.

Even with groceries and building supplies coming in by the ton, the barges still only had 120 days of ice-free travel. There was a railroad in Alaska, which ran from Seward to Fairbanks, but this did little to help the bush communities. Until the coming of the airplane, these villages were supplied by boats during the summer and dogsled during the winter—if they were supplied at all.

It was the airplane that brought Alaska into the twentieth century. Goods and people could travel farther faster, making the comforts of civilization available to even the most remote communities. Miners and trappers were assured of a consistent flow of goods and supplies in as well as the fruits of their labor out. Mail, which had formerly taken ten weeks to travel from the Pacific Northwest to even the large bush communities, was now available in hours.

Flying by the Seat of Your Pants

THE GOLDEN AGE OF THE ALASKA BUSH PILOT LASTED from the end of the First World War to the beginning of the Second World War. This was an era of very little regulation by the federal government. Pilots did more or less as they pleased. The government body responsible for air safety, the Civil Aeronautics Administration (CAA), had only a few agents, and they were scattered all across Alaska. Thus the chances of getting caught with an unsafe airplane were slim. As a result, what is illegal today was commonplace then. Planes flew overloaded, pilots were sometimes drunk, and structural damage to the airplanes was fixed with wire, tape, and sometimes even tree branches.

From 1917 to 1941, rugged individuals known as bush pilots worked on the very edge of civilization. They faced inclement weather in frail aircraft with undependable engines and made spectacular landings on poor runways—when there were runways—as part of their daily routine. It was an age when men—and some women—truly flew "by the seat of their pants" to maintain the delicate lifeline to the miners, trappers, and residents of bush Alaska.

8

MARVEL CROSSON IN 1927. THERE WERE ONLY A FEW FEMALE PILOTS IN THE EARLY DAYS OF AVIATION. (PHOTOGRAPH COURTESY OF JIM RUOTSALA)

The first airplane in Alaska was the *Tingmayuk.* (*Tingmayuk* is the Eskimo word for "bird.") The *Tingmayuk* was a bizarre contraption of 500 pounds of light wood, muslin, and piano wire. Built by "Professor" Henry Peterson, a Nome music teacher, the *Tingmayuk* was also probably the first airplane in history to be outfitted with skis. The inaugural flight was scheduled for May 9, 1911. On that fateful day, Professor Peterson had the plane pulled out of a shed and dragged to a smooth place on the tundra. Then he climbed aboard and turned on the biplane's gasoline engine. The propeller turned and the plane began inching forward. Unfortunately, that was all it did. When the plane failed to lift off from the level ground, it was taken to a nearby hill and given a push. However, even with a sliding start there was not enough airspeed to get the biplane aloft. The next day, the *Nome Nugget* reported "Peterson Unable to Defy the Law of Gravity," and that ended Alaska's first brush with "the aviation."

Alaskans were introduced to actual flying two years later. Three Alaskan businessmen contacted James V. Martin, a New Englander temporarily residing in Seattle, to fly over the ballpark during Fairbanks's Fourth of July celebration. Martin shipped his aircraft north by steamship to Skagway and then placed the flimsy craft on a railroad flatcar. It was hauled by rail to Whitehorse on the White Pass and Yukon Railroad and then went down the Yukon by barge to the Tanana River and Fairbanks. There was no way the Fairbanks businessmen could have predicted the immense success of this first Alaskan air show. Hundreds of people jammed the ballpark, sat on rooftops, or lined the streets as Martin circled over the town at the fantastic altitude of 200 feet. He flew for eleven minutes and then touched down, completing the first flight in Alaska.

In 1920, an event took place that would place Alaska in the aviation book of firsts. On July 15, five officers and three enlisted men from the U.S. Army took off from the East Coast of the United States on the first international cross-country flight in history. Commanded by Captain St. Clair Streett, a World War I combat pilot, the squadron entered the Territory of Alaska via Wrangell, crossed over Canada with a stop in Whitehorse, and then went on to Nome. The crew's

10

ALASKA'S FIRST AIRPLANE, THE TINGMAYUK. "PROFESSOR" HENRY PETERSON AND HIS HOME-
MADE AIRPLANE, BUILT WITH 500 POUNDS OF LIGHT WOOD, MUSLIN, AND PIANO WIRE, WERE "UN-

11

ABLE TO DEFY THE LAW OF GRAVITY" WHEN HE TRIED TO FLY ON MAY 9, 1911. (PHOTOGRAPH COURTESY OF JIM RUOTSALA)

*CAPTAIN AND MRS. J. V. MARTIN WITH THE FIRST PLANE TO SUCCESSFULLY FLY IN ALASKA.
TRANSPORTED NORTH BY STEAMSHIP AND FLATCAR, IT MADE AN ELEVEN-MINUTE FLIGHT OVER
FAIRBANKS ON THE FOURTH OF JULY, 1913. (PHOTOGRAPH COURTESY OF JIM RUOTSALA)*

arrival in Nome completed the flight and marked the first time that
the North American continent had been flown by humans.

Aviation came to Alaska to stay in 1922 in the form of Carl Ben
Eielson. He arrived in Fairbanks to take a job as a schoolteacher, but
flying was in his blood. He had served with the U.S. Army Corps
during the First World War and was struck with the possibility of
using airplanes to serve the miners, trappers, and villages scattered
across Alaska. In those early days of flying in Alaska, the dependable
money was in mail delivery. In 1922, a contract to carry the mail was
as good as gold.

After badgering postal authorities in Washington, D.C., for more than two years, Eielson was able to convince them to give him a contract to carry mail between Fairbanks and McGrath, a small mining community with a trading post about 250 miles west of Fairbanks. The U.S. Postal Service shipped Eielson a modified De Havilland airplane that, with the help of some friends and mechanics, he assembled on a Fairbanks baseball diamond.

Finally he was ready to fly. At 8:50 A.M. on February 21, 1924, Eielson lifted off from the ballpark and headed into the crisp Alaskan winter. It was five below zero on the ground. Since Eielson was flying in an open cockpit, it was substantially colder flying at eighty miles an hour above the snow-shrouded Alaskan interior.

It was a short flight. At 11:40 A.M. Eielson bounced to a stop on the frozen surface of the Kuskokwim River, completing the first air-

MEMBERS OF THE BLACK WOLF SQUADRON WHO, IN JULY 1920, COMPLETED THE FIRST INTERNATIONAL CROSS-COUNTRY FLIGHT. (PHOTOGRAPH COURTESY OF JIM RUOTSALA)

14   *ALASKA'S FIRST MAIL FLIGHT, BY CARL BEN EIELSON IN FEBRUARY 1924. (PHOTOGRAPH COURTESY OF JIM RUOTSALA)*

mail delivery in Alaskan history. There had been a brief but telling moment when Fred Milligan, who had the dogsled mail contract between Fairbanks and McGrath, looked up in surprise as Eielson flew over. "The pilot leaned out and waved at me with his long, black, bearskin mittens," Milligan remembered, and at that moment he knew his days on the dogsled mail run were over. It took Milligan twenty days to reach McGrath, a trip that Eielson would complete in a few hours. "I decided then and there," Milligan later recounted, "that Alaska was no country for dogs." Milligan quit dogsledding and went into the airline business, eventually working for Pan American.

Eielson dropped off his load of mail for McGrath and then collected the sixty pounds of letters and packages to be delivered to Fairbanks. But he made a crucial mistake: he turned off his engine.

As he socialized in McGrath, his engine cooled, and when he tried to restart the aircraft, the motor refused to turn over. It took three hours to get the De Havilland started again; so the Fairbanks-bound mail arrived three hours late, a delay that some say the U.S. Postal Service has never made up.

The 1920s: The Age of Experimentation

MANY ALASKANS HAD BEEN INTRODUCED TO FLYING in the U.S. Army and realized the airplane was clearly suited for Alaska. Enterprising pilots figured that they could now deliver supplies and passengers to the most remote parts of the territory. Most Native villages, mining camps, and trapline cabins were hundreds of miles from the nearest railroad. Supplies were being sent by riverboat and dogsled, but the airplane could bring cargo and mail to their destination in a matter of hours, not days.

At first the bush planes were used on a charter basis. A mining operation out of Cordova might need a piece of machinery and contract with a local pilot. If the pilot was lucky, the machinery would be light enough so that he could airlift it in one piece. If not, he had to dismantle the machine and take it in parts. If the machine still could not fit, the pilot might have to cut his plane so that the item could go inside. After the machinery had been delivered, the pilot would repair his plane.

Keeping mining operations supplied was profitable, because the companies regularly needed everything from soda crackers to ball bearings. Pilots who could not land a long-term contract operated on routes established by need. A pilot might hop to three or four villages, picking up and dropping off passengers and cargo along the way. The bulk of the cargo went to larger villages, but passengers could come from anywhere. A trapper might radio to be picked up at a bend of a river, or a Native might want to be picked up at a fishing camp. Specialty items like fresh fruit, a machine part, or a live turkey for Thanksgiving added to the mix of cargo the bush pilots carried.

As flying became more attractive, established air routes developed where the business existed, usually between the hubs and the larger bush communities. Pilots would live in a transportation hub and fly cargo and passengers where they needed to go. Juneau became the hub for southeast Alaska, while Anchorage was the hub for south-central Alaska. Fairbanks, which sits in the center of the interior, was a base for flight services as far east as Canada, as far north as Barrow and the Arctic Ocean, and west to the Bering Sea.

This golden age was a wild time, with pilots stealing each other's passengers and cargo or sending their competitors off on wild-goose chases. Archie Ferguson of Kotzebue, who ran the flying service farthest north, was famous for stealing passengers. He would be in the air and hear on the radio that someone in Selawik was asking for Jack Jefford. Archie would beat Jefford into Selawik and tell the passenger that Jefford had "cracked up in Deering." It would only be later that the passenger would realize that he or she had been fooled by the crafty Archie Ferguson.

Archie, it should be added, was also very good at keeping other pilots from stealing his passengers. His wife, Hadley, operated the radio, using a code; if a passenger was to be picked up in Deering, for instance, she would say the person was waiting in Shungnak. Anyone trying to steal Archie's passenger could burn a lot of fuel getting to Shungnak only to discover he had been fooled.

In some ways, passenger service in Alaska in the 1920s and 1930s was quite different from what it is today. Whether people liked to fly or not, they flew. They did not have a choice. But many aspects of bush flying remain the same. Then, as today, many passengers flew

17

18

ARCHIE FERGUSON, DUBBED "THE CRAZIEST PILOT IN THE WORLD" BY THE SATURDAY EVE-NING POST. THIS PORTRAIT OF FERGUSON HANGS IN THE LIBRARY AT THE UNIVERSITY OF ALASKA, FAIRBANKS. (PHOTOGRAPH COURTESY OF REEVE ALEUTIAN AIRWAYS)

on a "call and wait" basis. Passengers would call for their favorite pilot and wait until he or she showed up. There was a great deal of loyalty to pilots—until something went wrong. Then the loyalty would switch to another carrier. Pilgrim Springs on the Seward Peninsula had a Catholic boarding school; in the late 1930s they would only fly with Hans Mirow's airline. But that was only until one of Mirow's pilots, Jack Jefford, crashed while taking off. After that, the boarding school people would only fly with Wien Airlines, run by the four Wien brothers. The turnover rate for pilots well into the 1950s was high. Often a pilot who had been in Nome in the spring was not there in the fall. He might be flying in another part of the territory; he might be in a hospital, or even dead.

When a pilot did leave the area, it was not always easy for his replacement to win the loyalty of the old customers. Fred Chambers, a *cheechako* (tenderfoot) pilot in 1939, learned that when he cracked up in Buckland. He was doing fine until he hit a rut in the runway and knocked off one side of the landing gear. When he got back to Nome, his boss, Hans Mirow, told him, "You've still got your job, but I don't know if people will ride with you."

Mirow was right, Chambers learned. Mirow Flying Service would get a call to pick someone up at a mining camp and Chambers would fly out to pick them up. But, recalled Chambers, "they'd see me taxiing and they'd turn around and walk back to camp."

Finding pilots was hard, finding good ones close to impossible. Because of the distance to the Lower 48, particularly from the Arctic, pilots were hired by wire. In those days "when you hired a new pilot you knew it was going to cost you a new airplane," Chambers noted. That was part of the price of doing business in Alaska. You put a new pilot on payroll and pretty soon he was going to "wash out an airplane. You couldn't afford to fire him then because he had learned a valuable lesson at your expense."[2]

But flying was dangerous even for the most experienced pilots. Being on a plane that went down was not a common occurrence, but it was not unusual either. Weather conditions, aviation fuel quality, age of engine parts, and the pilot's experience and degree of fatigue

19

20

FRED CHAMBERS IN THE 1930S. THE TWO "PIPES" RUNNING UP TO THE CANVAS-
COVERED ENGINES ARE USED TO HEAT THE ENGINES SO THEY WILL START IN COLD
WEATHER. (PHOTOGRAPH COURTESY OF JIM RUOTSALA)

were all factors in keeping a plane aloft. If there was weakness in any one component, the plane could come down. Many did and many people died.

When planes did go down, pilots went to extraordinary lengths to retrieve the damaged craft. Planes were expensive, and it was often more economical to rebuild a damaged aircraft than buy a new one. Considering that a crashed plane was usually in a remote location, salvaging it meant flying a mechanic to the site to do just enough work to get the plane back in the air.

It was not an easy job for the mechanic. It meant camping in a tent at the crash site for weeks. In addition to the grueling work, the mechanics also had to put up with inquisitive bears, meandering moose, and mosquitoes that were "pretty near big enough to fly away with yuh," mechanic Jim Hutchison remembered of the weeks he spent in the bush to repair one particular plane. "I had to use newspapers under my clothes to keep the mosquitoes from biting."[3]

Archie Ferguson is on record as having one of the more difficult recoveries. After he had gone down on the Hogg River, fellow Kotzebue bush pilot John Cross told him: "That's one airplane, by God, you'll never fly again."

"Oh, yeah?" snapped Archie, who took every challenge seriously. To prove Cross wrong, he put together a rescue mission of twenty Eskimos and seventy-two dogs to drag the airplane almost 300 miles back to Kotzebue, where he had it repaired. It did fly again.

The competition for cargo and passengers was fierce and the rivalry sometimes led to brutal incidents. The sabotaging of landing strips, for instance, was not unknown. Archie Ferguson's chief competitor was Wien. They viewed each other as rivals, and Archie was not above adjusting the landing strips when he knew that one of the Wien brothers was on his way in. In these early days, landing strips were anything but convenient. Some were just level strips of land set aside for planes. Others were stretches of beach where someone in the village had stamped out giant letters reading "HARD," indicating that a landing was possible. Winter airstrips were stretches of ice that had been bulldozed level and framed with a dozen flare pots to

21

ARCHIE FERGUSON'S DOWNED PLANE ON THE HOGG RIVER. A RECOVERY MISSION OF SEVENTY-TWO DOGS AND TWENTY ESKIMOS HAULED THE PLANE MORE THAN 300 MILES BACK TO KOTZEBUE FOR REPAIRS. (PHOTOGRAPH COURTESY OF ED YOST)

distinguish the landing area from the rest of the floe. Flare pots, the "landing strip lights," were usually just coffee cans full of burning diesel.

During the day, flags stuck in the snow by villagers marked the runway. But even so, pilots had to be careful. Archie Ferguson once moved the landing strip flags so the next pilot in, Sig Wien, had a very rough landing. After that, Sig gave every landing strip a very careful look before he landed, particularly if he knew Archie had been in the area recently.

But landing was just one of the risks of flying. Sometimes pilots took off with wheels and found they needed skis to land; or took off with pontoons and found they needed wheels. "Mudhole" Smith once landed on rocks with skis and Merle Sasseen landed on a golf course with cables from a child's swing wrapped around his landing gear. After a number of such bad landings, Sasseen, known as much for his sense of humor as his flying, was filling out CAA paperwork on his crashes when he came to the question "General Ability as a Pilot?" Sasseen thought for a moment and then wrote, "I used to think I was pretty good, but lately I've begun to wonder."

There were probably only about fifty people who made their living as bush pilots in the 1920s. It was a precarious living. Planes and fuel were expensive. Big cargo contracts were few and far between. Revenues in those days were made in three ways: passengers, cargo, and mail. Passengers made up the bulk of the pilot's income, with cargo coming in second and mail third. Cargo was not a big money-maker, because most of the goods bought in the bush came in by barge once a year. Since airlifting supplies was expensive, bush residents often went without an item rather than pay the high cost of flying it in. Mail contracts were highly prized because they were government contracts. The U.S. government did pay, though it took months to actually get a check. Unfortunately there was not that much mail, so the government checks were not that large.

Pilots had to face other problems as well. Besides the upkeep of the plane there was the never-ending problem of fuel. Few communities had fuel tanks of any kind, so all combustibles—including airplane fuel, cooking fuel, fuel oil, and gasoline—came in fifty five-gallon barrels, which were taken off the barge and stored near the river. This made it easy to service boats that came upriver from the small villages, and airplanes that landed on the water. If the community had an airstrip, the fifty-five-gallon drums could be loaded onto a truck and driven out to the airplane.

There were no automatic pumps in those days, so the airplane fuel had to be pumped by hand. The cap on the top of the barrel was removed and a hand pump installed. Then the pilot would lever the

23

pump handle and force the fuel into his plane's gas tanks. Experienced pilots carried their own chamois to filter aviation gas.

But because many of the tanks were left outside, exposed to the weather, the labels on the barrels quickly wore off and the paint was stripped away. Since the drums were all stored together, a careless operator might mistake fuel oil for airplane fuel. Or if the pilot wasn't familiar with the operation of an airplane, he might think that gasoline was airplane fuel. There were other matters of concern, too. If the airplane fuel drum was left open, water could get into the fuel. Just as bad, mosquitoes and dust could get into the liquid and bring the plane down. One of the strangest airplane crashes in Alaska happened to John Cross of Kotzebue. Cross had to land on the tundra because his engine suddenly quit. When a claims adjuster examined the plane's engine, he discovered that a ball of dead mosquitoes had clogged the fuel system. After the corpses of the mosquitoes were removed, the engine worked perfectly.

Perhaps the most visible reminder of this age of aviation is the fifty-five-gallon drum. These drums were light enough to be lifted by two or three men and transported in a truck or airplane. When they were empty, they could be refilled anywhere fuel was available. Over the years so many were abandoned in remote parts of Alaska that today the fifty-five-gallon drums are nicknamed Alaskan daisies because, as the old saying goes, "they sprout everywhere."

• • • • • • • • • • • • •

If there was a pilot who could symbolize this early era, it was Archie Ferguson. Everyone who met Archie knew everything about him because Archie would tell them. If you didn't know something, Archie would tell you about it whether he knew about it or not. And how he loved to talk. Whether he was on the ground or in the air, he was talking, talking, talking. While many of the early bush pilots had sterling reputations, Archie Ferguson was known throughout the northland as Alaska's worst pilot — and possibly the "craziest pilot in the world," as he was dubbed by the *Saturday Evening Post.* "Maybe he's a pilot," other bush pilots said sadly of Archie, "but he shouldn't be."

Archie Ferguson was a sight to behold. As a young man in Kotzebue, he was five foot four and lean, but by the end of the 1930s he was built like a potato. His voice was high-pitched and when he laughed, which was often, he cackled like Donald Duck. He had only a few teeth left by the Second World War and kept his dentures in his back pocket—which was a mistake, because in one of his crashes, his teeth bit him.

Archie flew primarily in the Arctic, making cargo and passenger runs from Fairbanks to Nome, Kotzebue, and every village in be-

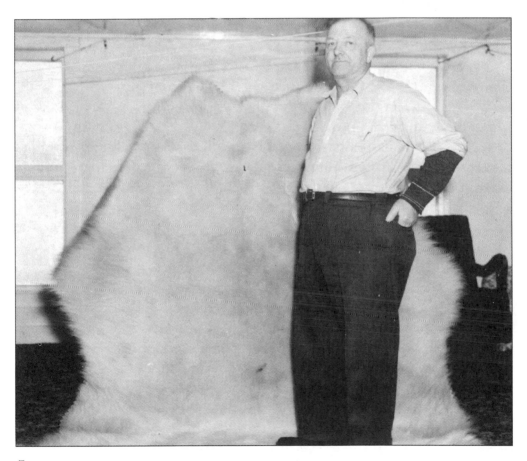

25

ARCHIE FERGUSON IN THE 1950s, STANDING IN FRONT OF A POLAR-BEAR-SKIN RUG. (PHOTO-GRAPH COURTESY OF EDITH R. BULLOCK)

tween. He had survived more crack-ups than any four pilots combined—as many as two dozen by the Second World War—and he walked away from every one of them. His flying was unorthodox, unpredictable, and a joy to watch—from the ground.

The best-known of Archie's ongoing escapades was the "Arctic bump." As far as Archie was concerned, a trip without excitement was a trip not worth taking, and he was very good at making his own excitement. On trips across the Arctic Circle he would tell newcomers that there was no air over that theoretical line on the earth.

"We're comin' ta the Arctic Circle!" he would yell at his passengers as he surreptitiously turned off his gas. "Ya can't see it but ya'll sure know when we hit it. The engine'll quit! There's no air in that darn circle for eight hundred feet!"

The plane's engine would then sputter and die and the plane would fall for hundreds of feet, the passengers shrieking in terror. After he had his laugh, Archie would quietly switch the fuel back on, restart the engine, and continue on his way.

Today, Alaska's pilots keep this tradition alive. While they don't allow the plane to fall hundreds of feet, they will give the plane an extra blast of fuel to make it "bump" when they come to the Arctic Circle.

• • • • • • • • • • • • •

Alaska's bush pilots made an international mark in aviation during this era as well. Hubert Wilkins came north in 1928 and convinced Carl Ben Eielson to join him in his quest to be the first to fly around the Polar Basin. Eielson agreed, and the trip almost cost both men their lives. The pair left Barrow in a Lockheed Vega on April 15, 1928, and followed the curvature of the earth toward Greenland. Twenty hours and twenty minutes later—after the longest nonstop airplane flight in the Arctic so far—they were forced to land near Spitzbergen because of storm conditions. For five days the men sat in their Vega waiting for the weather to lift. When it did, the snow was so deep the plane could not take off. Marooned hundreds of miles from any help, the men might have joined the ranks of those

SIR HUBERT WILKINS (LEFT) AND CARL BEN EIELSON IN POINT BARROW, ALASKA, SHORTLY BEFORE THEY BECAME THE FIRST PEOPLE TO CIRCUMNAVIGATE THE POLAR BASIN IN APRIL 1928. (PHOTOGRAPH COURTESY OF THE ALASKA RAILROAD COLLECTION/ANCHORAGE MUSEUM OF HISTORY AND ART)

who had flown off into the Arctic and never returned. But luck was on their side.

After they had stamped out a crude runway, Wilkins tried pushing the plane to get it started. He was successful but could not make it aboard when the plane took off. Eielson landed and they tried again. And again. On the third try, Wilkins was able to give the Vega enough of a push to get it started down the runway and, at the same time, hook his leg in the entry hatch of the plane. As the plane was taking off he levered himself aboard with a piece of driftwood he had picked up from a nearby beach. Considering that the Vega was low on fuel when the men were forced down, it is quite likely that had they not made it into the air when they did, they would not have had enough gas to reach a refueling station. When they completed their trip, they had traveled 2,200 miles around the Polar Basin, becoming the first people to do so.

While exploration was great for press headlines, it did not keep food on the pilot's table. Flying was a business and the pilot had to show a profit. Just as important as flying passengers was transporting cargo. Just as it is now, in the 1920s bush cargo was a mix of products, some living and some so bulky it had to be taken apart to fit inside. If the plane was too full, pilots sometimes lashed cargo on the outside. Sig Wien remembered flying a bedspring outside his plane. Other pilots had horror stories of timber and pipe that had to be strapped to the fuselage of their planes. Some photos of early aircraft show them so bulky with cargo strapped to the outside that it was a wonder the planes ever lifted off at all. Once the craft was in the air, it is surprising that the pilot could see over the cargo tied to the front.

Bush pilots could and would transport anything. Transporting walrus to zoos in the Lower 48 was not unusual. "They'd cry real tears when they'd be aboard because they were stressed, and it just hurt your feelings," remembered "K" Doyle, the first stewardess for Wien Alaska Airlines. Horses and dogs were not uncommon in the larger planes, and once in the 1950s Wien Alaska Airlines flew an elephant to Nome (in a larger cargo plane).

The proper loading of cargo was critical to the balance of the plane. Strapping down the cargo was important as well. Russ Merrill, for whom Merrill Field in Anchorage is named, learned about shifting cargo the hard way. He left Anchorage in a Whirlwind Travel Air on September 16, 1929, with a compressor for a gold mine. He never returned. The only clue as to what happened was a piece of fabric found floating in Cook Inlet and identified as being from his airplane. It was speculated that the compressor had shifted while he was in flight and the imbalance sent the plane tumbling into the inlet.

Archie Ferguson, of course, had his own cargo stories. Once in the 1920s, he alleged, he flew a load of turkeys from Nome to Kotzebue.

IN SEPTEMBER 1960, NORTHERN CONSOLIDATED AIRLIFTED FORTY-THREE REINDEER OFF NUNI-
VAK ISLAND ON THE FIRST LEG OF THEIR JOURNEY TO BECOME "ASSISTANTS" TO SANTA CLAUSES
ACROSS THE UNITED STATES. (PHOTOGRAPH COURTESY OF THE ANCHORAGE MUSEUM OF HIS-
TORY AND FINE ART)

He couldn't get the turkey crates into his Cessna Airmaster, so he
took the turkeys out of the crates and put them into his cargo hold
individually. Then, said Archie, he had trouble taking off, so he began
waving his hand in the cargo bay behind him. This upset the turkeys
and they started flying around in the back of the plane. This enabled
Archie to take off. Once aloft, Archie kept waving his hand to keep
some of the turkeys in flight all the time and was able to make it all
the way to Kotzebue without incident. While this is certainly a hu-
morous story, the fact of the matter is that domesticated turkeys don't
fly. But then again, a lot of bush pilots said Archie couldn't fly either.

The 1930s: The Age of Equipment

BY THE END OF THE 1920s, THE AVIATION BUSINESS was profitable enough to attract more pilots into the industry. But there was now a new breed of pilot. While many of the original class of bush pilots had grown up in Alaska, the new pilots came from Outside. Many of them had years of flying experience. But it was flying experience in the Lower 48, not in Alaska.

Once in Alaskan skies, these newcomers quickly learned what the seasoned Alaskan bush pilots already knew. It was a "long way between places" with few spots to set the plane down in case of emergency. Navigation equipment was still primitive. Days were short above the Arctic Circle during winter. Accurate maps were rare, except for nautical charts, which were only useful if a pilot was flying along the coastline.

The newer pilots also had to learn that many of the basic rules of navigation were different in Alaska. In the Arctic the sun didn't rise in the east during the winter; it came up in the south. Compass readings changed as well. Magnetic north and "true north," which were virtually the same to a pilot in Arizona or Louisiana, were substantially different to an aviator in the Arctic. The farther north the pilot flew, the greater the disparity between the two points grew. In Fairbanks, for instance, the difference between magnetic north and true north is 27 degrees. If a pilot flew by compass alone, he could be hundreds of miles off course by the end of the day. For example, imagine a pilot in the Lower 48 using only a compass as he flies from New Orleans to St. Louis. If there were a 27-degree difference between magnetic north and true north he would arrive in Atlanta thinking it was St. Louis. Then he would wonder how he could possibly be in Atlanta when he was following his compass "north" to St. Louis.

Then there was the weather. Southeast Alaska is famous for a violent wind called the *taku.* During the winter, wind from the Pacific Ocean blasts up the narrow channels of southeast Alaska. As the wind is funneled it grows in strength, with gusts of well over one hundred miles an hour, strong enough to blow cars over, sink ships, and make flying extremely dangerous. Along the Aleutian Islands, there is a powerful wind called a williwaw. The williwaw is particularly dangerous because it often rises from calm skies. One moment the weather appears clear and calm; the next, a 100-knot wind is blasting across an island. This is particularly dangerous for an airplane that is landing. In the rest of Alaska, wind shears are not uncommon, thick rain can cut visibility to zero, and low-lying fog can obscure coastlines.

The most experienced pilots from the Lower 48 quickly learned to adjust their flying to the weather. Many pilots use the power of the wind to their advantage. If the wind is constant over the landing strip, the pilots will face their planes into the wind and then cut back on the power. As they cut back on more and more power, the plane will gently settle to the ground. Conversely, on takeoff, the pilots will position the plane with the wind behind it and add just enough power to rise off the ground vertically. Under these conditions it is possible to take off using zero feet of runway!

But it was flying during the winter that separated the professionals from the amateurs. The brutal Alaskan climate forced pilots to develop new ways of thinking about flying. In Anchorage and Fairbanks, there could be snow on the ground as early as the middle of

October and as late as mid-May. Many pilots could not stand the cold and the flying conditions that winter brought; they fled south as soon as the lakes and streams began to freeze over.

Along with snow and ice came extremely low temperatures, particularly in the Arctic and the Interior. Even the most experienced pilots considered the cold an enemy of the aircraft. Cold affected the plane, its flying ability, and, most notably in Fairbanks, landing conditions.

Fairbanks sits in a geologic bowl—a low valley surrounded by hills. On many winter days temperature inversions make it far colder at ground level than at 12,000 feet. Under normal conditions, the air gets colder the higher a plane flies. But when there is a temperature inversion, the coldest weather is on the ground. A pilot might be flying in a temperature of ten below zero at 2,000 feet, but, as he descended, the plane would drop into a thick cold blanket of air over the landing strip, which could be at fifty degrees below zero. While the pilot, in the relatively warm cockpit, might not register the change in temperature, the plane's engine most certainly would.

32

"On the air-cooled engines," remembered Robert Jacobson, a mechanic and pilot for Alaska Airlines and MarkAir until his retirement in 1985, "the engine would sometimes freeze. Here you were coming in for a landing and the engine would quit on you at a hundred feet. If you weren't lined up for a landing, you were dead."[4]

Jacobson solved this problem with a bit of new technology. In the late 1940s he invented a cowling flap system that forced cold air to circulate around the hot engine before it was used to cool the engine. Only in Alaska, he noted, would you have to heat the air before you used it for cooling.

Cold weather also brought on the problem of icing, which occurs when moisture in the air comes into contact with an airplane and turns to ice. This usually happens when there is a temperature inversion. Under these conditions, the air is warmer in the clouds than on the ground. This kind of weather can be fatal to an unwary pilot. Imagine a pilot flying at 5,000 feet, where it is raining. When he drops to 3,000 feet he discovers that the temperature is below freezing. All the rain that was on his plane is now ice, and freezing rain from the

5,000-foot level would coat his plane thicker and thicker with ice. With each passing moment, the plane picks up weight. It may become too heavy to remain aloft, and will tumble out of the sky.

Archie Ferguson learned this lesson the hard way. Heavily loaded and icing up, he clipped a tree on the Hogg River.

"That was certainly close," his passenger muttered.

"Sure was," replied Archie, peering through his windshield, "but those two trees up there are the ones that are going to stop us." He pointed ahead to a pair of trees coming up fast.

As Archie predicted, his plane, overloaded with cargo on the inside and ice on the outside, hit the trees and tumbled to the ground.

Today, all passenger planes and most private planes are equipped with de-icing equipment. This equipment includes an alcohol-and-water mixture used on the windshield to keep it clear. This mixture is also allowed to trickle down the propellers from the hub. As the prop spins, the alcohol-and-water mixture covers the blades and maintains an ice-free surface on the rotor. For the wings, inflatable sections are installed on the leading edge, where icing usually starts. Before ice builds, the inflatable sections are pressurized, causing the front of the wing to expand. After ice forms, the tubes are deflated and the ice breaks free. Then, as ice forms on the deflated tubes, they are inflated, again breaking the ice free. This process continues as long as the plane is in danger of icing up.

One of the best-known pilots of the golden age was Harold Gillam. He was the embodiment of the ideal Alaska bush pilot, a dashing, handsome man with rugged features and a personality to match. Once, when some schoolchildren were asked to write a poem about their favorite person, a third-grader in Cordova wrote five lines that became Gillam's nickname for life:

He thrill 'em
Chill 'em
Spill 'em
But no kill 'em
Gillam

34

HAROLD "THRILL 'EM, CHILL 'EM, SPILL 'EM, BUT NO KILL 'EM" GILLAM. (PHOTOGRAPH COURTESY OF ROBERT C. REEVE COLLECTION/REEVE ALEUTIAN AIRWAYS)

Gillam started in the flying business in 1931 as part of the cargo supply line from Cordova to dozens of mining operations in the nearby mountains. His was a risky operation on the best of days. Cordova sits on a flat plain surrounded on three sides by steep mountains. On the fourth side is Orca Bay, which connects with the Gulf of Alaska. Turbulent winds and fog are common in the area, and storm clouds are considered a normal weather pattern. Adding to a pilot's woes, most of the landing strips at the mines were very short; some were just areas that had been dug out of the mountainside with bulldozers. Landing and taking off were treacherous. "If you undershot," the seasoned bush pilots said of the area, "you ran into a bluff. When you took off you hadn't a foot to spare."

But even in this country, it appeared that nothing could keep Gillam on the ground. One night "Honest John" McCreary fell in his cellar and was badly gouged by a nail. There was a blasting snowstorm and those who attended his wounds believed that McCreary would die because there was no way to get him to the nearest doctor, at Kennecott 125 miles away. But the storm didn't bother Gillam. Loading McCreary into his airplane, the pilot battled driving winds and snow to get him to the doctor. When the doctor said that McCreary probably wouldn't last the night, Gillam went up again, flying back to Cordova to fetch McCreary's son and bring him to Kennecott. That night Gillam flew 375 miles through a driving snowstorm and cemented his reputation as a man with the eyes of a cat.

Gillam remained in Cordova for three years and then went north to Fairbanks, where his reputation as an aviation marvel continued to grow. He was best known for his night flying. Regardless of the weather, Gillam would rise in the evening, dress, and then fly to wherever he was scheduled to go. In 1938, Gillam had the mail contract between Fairbanks and twenty bush communities. For the previous few years these villages had been serviced by Pan American, but the mail had been delivered only when the weather was good. Gillam delivered the mail on time, month after month, season after season, with a perfect safety record. Gillam's record of on-time deliveries was so good that the U.S. Post Office declared it the best in the

HAROLD **G**ILLAM. (P*HOTOGRAPH COURTESY OF* R*OBERT* C. R*EEVE* C*OLLECTION/*R*EEVE* A*LEUTIAN* A*IRWAYS*)

United States and its territories—better than in places like Kansas or Arizona where the weather was more predictable and the terrain more suited to emergency landings.

Alaskan pilots accepted Gillam's flying exploits as fact, because they watched him perform feats of navigational wonder. But pilots from other parts of the country didn't believe a word about Gillam. In the mid-1930s, one man, Donneld Cathcart, was so sure that Alaskans were lying about Gillam's talents that he rode with Gillam between Fairbanks and Barrow.

Gillam fueled his Fairchild Pilgrim with seven hours' worth of fuel for the six-and-a-half-hour trip, and the two men scrambled aboard. As far as Cathcart could see, Gillam had no navigational equipment. The Pilgrim leaped into the air, chewed its way through several thousand feet of cloud cover, and proceeded to fly over a sea of clouds for six and a half hours. Then, without warning, Gillam nosed the plane back down into the cloud bank.

In the next instant the Pilgrim was enveloped in the clouds. Down and down the plane went, and no matter where he looked, Cathcart could see nothing but clouds in every direction. Suddenly he saw something flash by the Fairchild's windshield. It was the antenna poles marking the landing area on the Barrow Lagoon. Gillam made a perfect landing. Cathcart was forced to believe that Gillam's reputation was not only accurate but well earned.

Archie Ferguson was still flying at this time, and continued to add to his legacy. In the late 1930s, he was transporting two baby polar bears when they got loose in his aircraft. Archie didn't know the cubs were loose until one of them hit him on the back of his head. Everyone on the ground knew Archie was in trouble when he came on the air and began shrieking that bears were loose in his plane and were going to eat him alive. For the next twenty minutes, Archie kept everyone within radio range tuned in to his battle with the bear cubs. He landed in Kotzebue so perfectly that it was said by more than one of his competitors that one of the bears must have been at the controls.

A non-Alaskan pilot whose name is etched in the history of Alaskan aviation is Wiley Post. After the hubbub over Charles Lindbergh flying across the Atlantic to Paris in 1927, aviators set their sights on a new goal: a flight around the world. The *Graf Zeppelin* had circled the globe in twenty-one days but Wiley Post, even then a famed American aviator, estimated that he could do it by airplane in ten days. On June 23, 1931, Post and the Australian aviator Harold Gatty left Roosevelt Field, New York, in a Lockheed Vega named the *Winnie Mae.* Eight days, fifteen hours, and fifty-one minutes later the *Winnie Mae* landed after circumnavigating the earth in record time.

But Post felt he could do it even faster. Two years later, on July 15, 1933, the *Winnie Mae* left Floyd Bennett Field in New York. This time Post was flying alone. Using an automatic pilot, which he had invented, he flew nonstop to Berlin and proceeded across Russia and the Bering Sea. Once over Alaska he became lost in Alaska's legendary bad weather. Spotting a radio tower poking through the cloud

39

WILEY POST'S FAMED WINNIE MAE *IN* FLAT, ALASKA, 1933, ON HIS AROUND-THE-WORLD SOLO FLIGHT. (PHOTOGRAPH COURTESY OF JIM RUOTSALA)

cover, he landed on the rough 800-foot runway at the mining community of Flat. The moment he hit the airstrip he was in grave danger. The *Winnie Mae* nosed over on its prop and the landing gear on the right side snapped off.

Now, with Post's around-the-world-solo record in jeopardy, the miners of Flat rushed to his rescue. While Post got some badly needed sleep, the miners worked through the night to make what repairs they could and radioed for spare parts from Fairbanks. When the *Winnie Mae* was flyable, Post flew to Fairbanks for more extensive repairs. With the assistance of the miners at Flat and the mechanics in Fairbanks, Post was able to circle the globe alone in a record seven days, eighteen hours, and forty-nine minutes.

But Wiley Post left a grim legacy in the northland. In February 1935, he purchased a hybrid Lockheed Orion-Explorer and outfitted the craft with pontoons from another plane, a Fairchild 71. That August, American humorist Will Rogers joined Post for a leisurely flight to Alaska. The two men arrived in Fairbanks to refuel on their way to Barrow. With the Orion-Explorer tanks partially filled to let the plane take off from the waters of the Chena River, the two men left for Barrow.

40

By the early afternoon the men were lost above the cloud cover in one of the worst August storms in years. About 3:00 P.M. Post spotted some land and trees through a break in the clouds and dropped through the cloud cover. He followed a stream until it came to a lagoon large enough for the Orion to land. There was a small Eskimo fishing camp on the shore of the lagoon, where Post was given precise directions to Barrow, sixteen miles away. Post and Rogers talked for a moment and then disappeared back in the Orion. The plane took off and rose fifty feet off the water—and the engine quit. The plane took a nosedive into the lagoon and, in the next instant, both men were killed. Claire Oakpeha, one of the Eskimos on the lagoon, ran the sixteen miles to Barrow with the bad news. Later, Oakpeha would report that Rogers said only one thing to him as he stuck his head out of the Orion: "Anyone here from Paducah?" Other than his conversation with Post, those were Rogers's last words. What was particularly tragic was that Post and Rogers had died of pilot error:

WILEY *POST AND* W*ILL* R*OGERS (EMERGING FROM THE DOORWAY) IN* J*UNEAU,* A*LASKA, IN 1938.*
(P*HOTOGRAPH COURTESY OF* J*IM* R*UOTSALA*)

the plane had simply run out of gas. When the gas tanks were probed with a stick, they were found to be bone dry.

As Post and Rogers proved, flying could be deadly. Pilots had to be ever alert to changing circumstances, even if they were sure they were operating safely. Landings and takeoffs could be especially dangerous. In the late 1930s, Merle "Mudhole" Smith was flying for Cordova Air Service; one of his clients was the Bremner Mining Company. The mine was in a very inaccessible spot for an airplane: Its airstrip was 300 feet long and barely twenty feet wide; it had a ditch on each side; and it was covered with stones.

After a driving rainstorm, Smith arrived at the mine to drop off supplies. As he was loading up to return to Cordova, one of the miners advised him to check the landing strip to make certain that he had not dislodged any rocks when he landed. If he had, there would be a

MERLE "MUDHOLE" SMITH. (PHOTOGRAPH COURTESY OF THE ESTATE OF MERLE SMITH)

pothole in the runway, which would make his takeoff hazardous. Merle said he was sure he hadn't flipped any rocks large enough to be a danger, so checking the runway was not necessary.

He was wrong.

As he started to take off, the left wheel on his Stearman dropped into a mudhole that had formed after his tail wheel had dislodged a rock during the landing. The Stearman buckled and bounced nose down, the propeller boring into the ground at 1,800 revolutions a minute. Thereafter Merle Smith was known as "Mudhole" Smith.

Sometimes even the most prepared pilot could find himself in trouble. In southeast Alaska, Tony Schwamm was landing a plane on what he thought was deep water. His pontoons touched the water and he started to glide to a stop, when suddenly he felt himself being lifted skyward. When he looked out his side window he realized that his plane was on the back of a whale.[5] Once the whale realized it had a plane on its back, it submerged, leaving Schwamm with a story that will live forever in the annals of Alaska bush flying.

Another bush pilot who left his mark on Alaska aviation in the 1930s was Alex Holden of Alaskan Southern Airways. Though his career spanned many decades, Holden is most often remembered for what is laughingly called the Great Corpse Rush.

During the Great Depression a fisherman in Dutch Harbor died. A death certificate was issued by the U.S. Marshal and the next of kin was notified, thanks to some letters found among the old man's possessions. One of those documents was the fisherman's will, in which he left his entire estate, estimated at $1.5 million in 1995 dollars, to a niece in Washington State. She decided that his corpse should be transported back to Seattle.

The cadaver was 900 miles west of Seward, the closest ferry terminal; the woman offered several thousand dollars to any pilot who would fly to Dutch Harbor and bring the corpse to the ferry. During the Depression, a few thousand dollars could mean the difference between life and death for a small airline, so more than a few pilots tried to reach Dutch Harbor. The first to arrive was Alex Holden.

But as he quickly discovered, he got more than he'd bargained for.

ALEX HOLDEN STRAPPING A CORPSE TO HIS WING BECAUSE THE CADAVER WOULD NOT FIT INSIDE THE AIRPLANE. (PHOTOGRAPH COURTESY OF REEVE ALEUTIAN AIRWAYS)

The fisherman had died of "complicated internal conditions," which required that his remains be disposed of promptly. So the body had already been buried. To recover it, Holden would need an exhumation order. But there was no judge in Dutch Harbor. Holden wired his boss of the complications and asked for instructions. The reply he received was short and to the point: "Get the body."

Holden got an exhumation order from a judge in Anchorage by radio and had the body dug up. As quickly as possible he had it wrapped in a canvas shroud and several coats of shellac applied to seal in the corpse.

But after the shellac had dried, Holden discovered there was no way to slide the mummy into his plane. The cadaver couldn't be bent, and Holden couldn't maneuver the stiff cargo through the cargo door. Even if he had been able to cut a hole in the side of the airplane and slip the corpse in, the stench of shellac would have made the trip unbearable. After trying every cargo-loading trick he knew, Holden finally bowed to the inevitable and strapped the corpse onto the top of a wing and flew it to Seward.

The 1940s: The CAA Arrives

IF THERE WAS A DATE THAT MARKED THE END OF THE wild and woolly days of rough-and-tumble competition it was the fall of 1938. After years of loosely watching bush pilots, the CAA (the forerunner of today's Federal Aviation Administration, the FAA) decided to regulate the industry. Announcing that it intended to assign routes on the basis of "convenience and necessity," the CAA sent its inspectors to Alaska to see which routes should be assigned. This was a polite way of saying that the CAA was going to decide who had a monopoly on which routes.

The pilots were not pleased with the idea of regulation coming to Alaska and called a mass meeting to discuss the matter among themselves. This proved to be a bad idea. It was, reported Ray Petersen of Wien Consolidated Airline, "like a bunch of lions and panthers tossed in one case!"[6] For the first time, every pilot in Alaska was going to come face-to-face with every one of his competitors. As soon as all the pilots were in the same room they decided that their competitors were a greater threat to their livelihood than government regulations, and after some heavy drinking, a wild brawl erupted. That finished any hope of the pilots' standing as a solid front against the CAA. Just as the coming of barbed wire symbolized the end of the cowboy, the coming of the CAA ended the frontier days of the bush pilot.

After examining the routes, the CAA decided to assign airways on the basis of who had been flying there. If a pilot had been servicing an area for the period between May 14 and August 22, 1938, he would be assigned that service route. This "grandfathering" caught some of the pilots without a route. Though Bob Reeve had been flying in the Valdez area for years, during the three months the CAA chose as their window, he had been doing aerial mapping in Fairbanks. So Reeve didn't get a route. On the other hand, Ray Petersen had been working out of Bethel at the time and, because he had a girlfriend in Anchorage, he had been flying back and forth between the two communities frequently. So he got the Bethel-to-Anchorage route, "the only reason I had an airline," he later noted.[7]

The arrival of the CAA in Alaska was both a blessing and a curse. It was not so much that the CAA brought new technology to Alaska; rather, the organization brought a hard-nosed approach to federal regulations. Planes would not be allowed to fly overloaded. Every aircraft would have to maintain its equipment and engines to federal standards, and required equipment was routinely checked to make sure it worked. Pilots who installed broken equipment just to meet the federal requirements soon discovered that the CAA was serious about making every plane safe.

Along with that technology came a growing number of CAA inspectors. From the pilots' point of view, this was not a step forward. As far as they were concerned, the CAA was evil; they hated it with ferocity. Pilots saw the CAA not as a safety-oriented agency but as a bureaucracy full of incompetents intent on putting them out of business. The small airlines had their hands full just struggling to survive. Now the CAA was requiring them to keep books, maintain equipment, and not overload their planes.

The CAA was supposedly in Alaska to make sure the pilots flew safely. But the pilots felt that the way the agency enforced regulations

48

BOB REEVE (LEFT) AND PHOTOGRAPHER RUSSELL DOW. (PHOTOGRAPH COURTESY OF JIM RUOT-SALA)

ensured that almost no one could stay in business. As for the CAA's point of view, the inspectors were usually amazed at the condition of Alaskan airplanes. They wondered how these crates could even get off the ground, much less fly cargo and passengers. Many of the pilots were flying without radios or fire extinguishers. Overloading was common, equipment failure was frequent, and engine maintenance was slipshod.

Thus pilots played a cat-and-mouse game with the CAA, dodging the inspectors while the CAA tried to catch them unawares. If the matter had not been so serious, it would have been comical. When the CAA tried to pull a snap inspection in Kotzebue, every pilot who could fly had flown the coop by the time the inspector arrived. Whenever a plane crashed on takeoff, it was a race to see who got to it first: the CAA with a set of scales to weigh the cargo, or every other pilot on the airstrip. The pilot's buddies would be busy helping the unlucky airman unload his plane so the CAA inspector would not find that the plane had been grossly overloaded. Once Don Emmons went off the runway at Weeks Field in Fairbanks and by the time the CAA inspectors got there the only cargo left aboard was "about two cases of beans."[8]

Although the CAA had a rough time enforcing its hated regulations, the agency's activities did have a noticeable impact on flying in Alaska. Just as the state trooper who parks visibly along the interstate slows traffic simply by being there, the CAA changed aviation in Alaska just by showing a presence.

Sometimes pilots had good reason to ignore CAA regulations. The weight limits for legal loads were quite strict, and pilots carrying full tanks of fuel had a very narrow margin for cargo. Even Burleigh Putnam, who headed the CAA in Alaska during the 1940s, admitted that "payload didn't mean a thing. Our own CAA airplane, when it was full of gasoline, could only carry twenty pounds legally and I flew it one time with a 1,050-pound overload."[9]

Most pilots fudged on their poundage when they flew cargo loads. Even after the CAA moved maximums up to more reasonable levels, pilots continued to overload their airplanes. The reason for the fudg-

BURLEIGH PUTNAM'S STINSON SR-10. PUTNAM WAS THE HEAD OF THE CAA IN ALASKA DURING THE 1920S AND 1930S. (PHOTOGRAPH COURTESY OF JIM RUOTSALA)

ing: profit. The bigger the load, the greater the profit. Overloading was often not just a result of greed; it was a matter of keeping the airline companies in business.

Ray Petersen explained overloading in the early days:

> Our loads were determined by the length of the field and whether we could make it off the ground. We'd fill up all the seats, throw in all the freight our passengers' laps would hold, fill up the gas tanks, and take off. On a long trip we could take an extra load because as the gas burned out we got the additional lift we needed to make it over a pass. When the [CAA inspector] was around, we'd wait until he went to lunch, then everybody would overload their planes and take off fast.

But there was great danger in overloading. Many pilots thought they knew the safety limits and would throw in an extra box. After all, it

RAY PETERSEN. (*PHOTOGRAPH COURTESY OF JIM RUOTSALA*)

was only a box. The next time it was two boxes or a heavy bag. It was, as Ray Petersen noted, "that last ten bucks' worth of freight"[10] that killed the pilot. Maybe he needed more feet of runway than he had and went off the landing strip into the trees. Or he increased his stall speed so that he quite literally fell out of the sky on final approach.

Sometimes the plane had to be cut to accommodate the cargo. In the summer of 1949, polar bear hunter Harold Little watched as Archie Ferguson "jammed a boiler into his Fairchild 24. Archie wanted that boiler in his plane in the worst way. When the boiler wouldn't fit, Archie chopped a hole in the roof of the Fairchild and flew it with the stove pipe sticking through the top of the airplane."[11]

BEFORE THE DAYS OF FORKLIFTS AND CRANES, EVERYTHING WAS LOADED INTO PLANES BY HAND—EVEN OBJECTS AS HEAVY AND AWKWARD AS THIS BOILER. (PHOTOGRAPH COURTESY OF REEVE ALEUTIAN AIRWAYS)

Other tales of overloading also have a trace of humor. Mudhole Smith, known to be cantankerous upon occasion, once loaded up a plane and sent a young pilot, Ralph Westover, into the sky. "The plane was overloaded and packed with boxes from door to door," Westover recalled. He made it off the ground but when he returned, Mudhole was in a rage. "You had another hundred feet of runway," Mudhole snarled. "You could have taken another hundred pounds of cargo!"[12]

Before the 1950s, cargo meant revenue on small planes, so it went aboard first. Passengers often sat on top of the sacks and boxes. Many of the pilots preferred cargo to passengers because, as glacier pilot Bob Reeve put it succinctly, "cargo don't talk back."

Flying passengers was often financially risky for everyone concerned. If a pilot had to fly a carpenter out to a construction site, the carpenter often had to fly first and wait for his tools to catch up to him. This was terribly expensive for the construction company, because the carpenter could not work if he did not have his tools with him, yet he would still have to be paid since he was on the construction site. The news for the employer could get worse if the weather closed in. Then the carpenter would wait days and days for his tools. This set of circumstances did not endear the flying service to the construction company.

Sometimes the passengers could be the problem. Don Emmons was taking his common-law wife to Fairbanks when she apparently decided to commit suicide. Halfway to Fairbanks she opened the door and stepped out into thin air. At the last moment, another passenger caught her by the foot and held on tightly. However, since the woman was hanging lower than the wheels, Emmons had no choice but to order her dropped before he landed. She fell into a deep snowbank and was rescued by dogsledders shortly thereafter.

Bill Munz, flying out of Nome, even showed how an airplane could do double duty and help a dog team. In December 1945 he was north of Teller, flying a pregnant woman into Nome, when he spotted a herd of reindeer being chased by a runaway dogsled. He followed the coastline until he spotted Frank Ahnangatoguk stranded four miles

55

DON EMMONS. (*PHOTOGRAPH COURTESY OF JIM RUOTSALA*)

behind his dog team. Munz picked him up and then flew back to the dog team. There he "executed a treacherous landing between the dog team and the reindeer herd, thus stopping the team."[13] Ahnangatoguk got out, and Munz landed in Nome shortly thereafter. But by then he had an extra passenger on board: The pregnant woman had given birth before he made it to Nome.

While the dirty, rusted aircraft that flew in the Alaskan bush may have been considered primitive by many Lower 48 pilots, the planes were remarkably dependable. In the territory, a plane was not just a vehicle that moved people and cargo from one place to another. It was a lifeline and lifesaver. But it took more than a pilot to make the trip. Mechanics were as critical as the pilots. Quite a bit of sweat and precision went into maintaining the aircraft, from the engine block to the fuselage skin. When Walter Beech of Beechcraft was in Kotzebue in 1941 he told the Alaskan aviators that the stitch Eskimo women had done on the fabric of the planes in the Arctic was better than that done by machines in his factory! Beech also endeared himself to

Alaskans by his comment concerning the Travel Air, one of the most dependable planes in the sky. "Well, damn it all, I designed 'em right," he said in Cordova, "and they should still be flying."[14] Some of them are still flying today.

But all this technology did not translate into better flying conditions. The weather was still unpredictable. Arctic weather still closed in suddenly and remained unflyable for days. Sometimes good flying weather would self-destruct so quickly that pilots would be forced to land wherever they were and wait for the clouds to lift. Sometimes the pilots didn't get that chance. In the mid-1950s, Jack Jefford was flying between Golovin and Elim in northwest Alaska when he was caught in a powerful downdraft and suddenly felt "an awful jar on the airplane." Not sure what had happened, he began easing back on the throttle.

Nothing happened, so he eased back another increment.

Again he felt no difference in his flying, so he eased back on the throttle again.

He kept easing back on the throttle and feeling no effect until he

*R*USS *M*ERRILL'S *T*RAVEL *A*IR. (*P*HOTOGRAPH COURTESY OF *J*IM *R*UOTSALA)

realized that he could not possibly be flying. So he turned his engine off.

When the weather cleared he found himself perched on a mountaintop. There he stayed for seven days waiting to be rescued.

Archie Ferguson also had his problems with the weather. In December 1946, Ferguson was flying his neighbor, Bess Cross, back to Kotzebue. Following Archie was a second plane carrying Cross's $2,500 fur coat, a case of Scotch whisky, several pounds of pork chops, and a load of vegetables for Cross's store, the Kotzebue Trading Post.

As the two planes headed out along the Bering Sea coast, the second pilot lost Archie in the fog. Then a weather front moved in and the pilot was forced to land on a sandbar to wait for the cloud cover to pass. Seven days later, when Archie found him, the pilot was sitting bundled up in Cross's fur coat and guzzling her whisky. He had already devoured every one of her pork chops and all of the produce.

Until the end of the Second World War, most pilots did not use instruments. Today, there are two ways to fly: VFR (visual flight rules) and IFR (instrument flight rules). In the golden era of the bush pilots, most aviators flew by line of sight. When new instruments became available, the older pilots shied away from using them. If a *cheechako* asked an old bush pilot if he flew VFR or IFR, the pilot would sometimes jokingly say "IFR"—an acronym, to veteran pilots, for "I fly the river" or "I follow the railroad."

But technology, particularly in the form of navigation equipment, could keep the pilots alive. While folklore had it that Harold Gillam hadn't a nerve in his body, the fact was that he was doing more than flying by instinct. While most pilots flew by following dog trails in the snow or by using a pocket compass and a crude map, Gillam was a technology buff. Early in his career he established a network of radio stations on the ground in the areas where he flew, and trusted friends flicked them on whenever they knew Gillam was in the air. He also studied meteorology and weather maps and stayed current on state-of-the-art navigational aids. He installed and used a directional gyro, altimeter, direction finder, and other navigational tools that in the late 1930s were considered more magician's tricks than aviation mainstays. Gillam was adept at using his tools, and that was what kept him alive.

Jokes and antics aside, death was a pilot's constant companion. "You don't have to go up," the old saying goes, "but you do have to come down"; every pilot knew that whenever he went up, he might not have a choice of where, when, or how he was going to come down.

When Fred Chambers went missing on the Nulato River in January 1939, Hans Mirow and a score of other pilots went out looking for him. On the first day, Mirow was caught in a whiteout while following a wide swath cut in the forest for a telegraph wire. Mirow nicked some trees about eight miles from Kaltag and came down hard. It took rescuers several days to find his body. That was often the price of flying in the north.

Sometimes the living paid a high price, too. In February 1940,

CAA pilot Benton W. "Steve" Davis went down outside Cordova. He survived the crash but discovered that his foot was wedged beneath a panel. For the next twenty-four hours he sat helplessly as his foot froze. Finally he was able to retrieve his pistol and shoot his foot free. He lived, but it took time in the hospital for him to recover.[15]

The Golden Age of the bush pilot had come to an end. The pilots had flown as they wanted, charged what they could get away with, and thumbed their noses at the authorities. Then came the CAA with its rules and regulations. Soon, the world of the Alaska bush pilot was turned upside down.

6

The Thousand-Mile War

WORLD WAR II BROUGHT UNEXPECTED CHANGES TO
Alaska, even before the attack on Pearl Harbor. In March 1941, the
U.S. military decided to open an air corridor to Siberia. The U.S.S.R.
and Great Britain were fighting Adolf Hitler's Germany and they
needed American equipment and supplies, particularly airplanes. At
that point, the United States was neutral and wanted to remain that
way. But the United States also wanted to help its traditional friend,
Great Britain, and her allies. The United States resolved the problem
of staying neutral by designing a political program known as Lend-
Lease. While the United States would remain officially neutral, it
would "lend" or "lease" aircraft and supplies to Britain and the Soviet
Union, which would pay for the usage or loss after the war. Planes
on their way to England went via the East Coast, while aircraft on
their way to Russia went through Alaska. American pilots were not
allowed to fly the planes out of the United States, so they would fly
them to Alaska and turn them over to the Soviet crews, who would
then fly them out of the country.

Before the Alaska–Siberia route (ALSIB) was established, pilots flying to the Soviet Union traveled through the Middle East, putting 13,000 miles on the aircraft before they ever saw combat. ALSIB cut that distance to 3,000 miles. From September 1942 until the end of the war, Soviet crews received almost 8,000 fighters and bombers in Fairbanks, flew them to a small airfield a hundred miles north of Nome, and then took them across the Bering Sea to Siberia.

Once the United States was dragged into the Second World War, it no longer had to pretend to be neutral, and Lend-Lease ended. But this did not end Alaska's role as a front line of the war. While every American-history buff knows that the Japanese staged a surprise attack on Pearl Harbor in the Hawaiian Islands on December 7, 1941, few remember that the Japanese also bombed Alaska and actually landed on and controlled two islands in the Aleutian chain.

On June 3 and 4, 1942, two Japanese aircraft carriers with eighty-two planes launched a surprise air raid on Dutch Harbor in the Aleutians. An American PBY Catalina had spotted the invasion fleet before it actually arrived at Dutch Harbor, so it was not truly a surprise attack. The damage was substantial nonetheless.

After the initial bombing, the Japanese seized two of the western-most islands in the Aleutians, Attu and Kiska. This was the first time invaders had occupied American soil since the War of 1812. This was just as good for morale in Japan as it was bad for morale in the United States.

Attu and Kiska were key to the Japanese control of the airspace over the Pacific Ocean. With long-range airplanes based in Attu and Kiska, the Japanese air force could strike to the east at American forces in Alaska or attack American convoys crossing the Pacific to the south. Long-range Japanese fighter planes based on the island of Midway in the central Pacific could control all the parts of the Pacific that the planes from Attu and Kiska could not reach.

But there was one problem in this sequence of logic. The Battle of Midway, which took place at the same time as the bombing of Dutch Harbor, was a disaster for the Japanese. They lost four aircraft carriers, 275 airplanes, and more than 4,800 men. On a global scale, the Japanese lost the southern footing for their grand plan to control the airspace over the Pacific. The failure to take Midway effectively left the Japanese soldiers on Attu and Kiska with no mission to fulfill. But the troops remained on the island, primarily as a morale booster for the Japanese public and only secondarily as a fighting force that could be used to attack any Allied invasion fleet steaming across the Pacific.

Fortunately for Alaska, the invasion of the Japanese brought new meaning to the phrase "North to Alaska." Overnight, the U.S. military became aware of the danger of leaving an exposed northern flank, and the Pentagon began to pour millions of dollars in supplies and equipment into the northland. The Japanese had to be contained on the islands they occupied and, eventually, they had to be driven out. But that would take men and supplies.

The first problem to be faced was as old as Alaska: lack of transportation corridors. There was no road to Alaska, air cargo routes were indirect, barge traffic was slow, and weather stalled land, water, and air traffic for weeks at a time. The only reasonable way to move millions of tons of supplies into Alaska quickly was overland, so a road had to be built. In a little over nine months, under summer and winter conditions so severe that any other project would have stalled, the United States Army constructed the Alaska–Canada Highway, immediately known as the Al–Can and today as the Alaska Highway.

At the same time, supplies were pouring in by ship to the now rebuilt Dutch Harbor at the rate of 400,000 pounds a month. Thus began the air war dubbed the "Thousand-Mile War," referring to the length of the Aleutian chain of islands. With the Japanese flying east from their bases on Attu and Kiska and the Americans west from their supply bases in Kodiak and Dutch Harbor, the islands between Dutch Harbor and Attu were soon littered with the remains of Zeros, P-38s, B-25s, Airacobras, and Catalinas.

What neither side knew before the invasion but learned quickly was that the Aleutians were probably the worst place in the world to do battle. The islands were isolated from both Japan and North America by great distances across the turbulent North Pacific. Keeping men fed and equipment in top shape required a constant stream of cargo ships, which were easy targets for the airplanes of the other side. The Japanese on Kiska were taking such a heavy pounding from American bombers that they feared for their supply ships. As a result, they only shipped supplies for Kiska as far as Attu. From there the supplies were flown to Kiska.

The weather was another problem. Because the Aleutians divide the North Pacific from the Bering Sea, the islands are subject to violent storms when weather systems from the two oceans collide. As a result, the weather in the Aleutians is notoriously unpredictable. It can go from dead calm to a howling storm in a matter of minutes. The Aleutians were the only place in the world, pilots swore, where it was possible to have fog and a fifty-mile-an-hour wind at the same time. The wind could shift suddenly, or there could be two winds blowing in opposite directions immediately next to each other, or there could be no wind at all until a plane took off, when a hundred-mile-an-hour wind would come out of nowhere. It was not unusual for a plane to crab left against the wind as it began to accelerate for takeoff and then be forced to crab right halfway down the runway because there were two strong winds blowing in opposite directions across the runway. Other times pilots reported wind socks that showed the wind blasting east at one end of the runway, west at the other end, and dead calm in the middle. Sometimes the pilots had to fight headwinds so strong that it would take them six hours to reach their destination. On the return trip, with a tailwind, they could cover the same distance in two hours.[16] Pilots quickly learned that flying the Aleutians took a special skill: the ability to expect the unexpected.

Jokes about the weather—and particularly the cloud cover—were common. As more than one pilot said, you knew the cloud cover was too thick for flying "if you can't see your copilot." You could test for altitude in the fog by sticking your hand out the window. "If it touches a ship's mast," the saying went, "you're flying too low." One pilot lost in fog claimed to have followed a duck to safety because he knew that a duck would not fly into a mountain. Another pilot flying a PBY that was fighting the wind claimed that a seagull landed on

64

A *PBY CATALINA ALOFT OVER THE BERING SEA IN 1953. THE WIRE HANGING FROM THE REAR OF THE PLANE IS ABOUT TO "SNATCH" A LOAD OF MAIL. THE MAIL, IN A CANISTER, IS ATTACHED TO A*

CROSSLINE THAT IS RUN BETWEEN THE TWO FLAGS IN THE FOREGROUND. THE COAST GUARD CUTTER Northwind IS IN THE REAR. (PHOTOGRAPH COURTESY OF THE U.S. COAST GUARD)

his wing. If the weather was too thick for a seagull, it was too dangerous for a PBY, so the pilot set the plane down on the water. There the seagull jumped off his wing and swam away.

While Alaskan winters are legendary for their length and deep cold, the winter of 1942–43 was exceptionally harsh. Temperatures in the Alaskan Interior dropped to −67, and along the Aleutians it was so cold that blowtorches had to be used to warm airplane engines so they would start. It took hours to chip the ice off the planes. When the men weren't out in the cold working on the aircraft, they were shivering in their tents, where temperatures didn't rise above freezing for weeks at a time.

The Aleutian soil was another problem. Because the islands were part of the so-called ring of fire, the ring of volcanic activity around the Pacific Rim, much of the earth was dark brown or black and covered with partly decayed plant matter known as muskeg. With men and equipment moving on it, the muskeg bog turned to a muddy soup. Often the men building roads or airstrips were up to their knees in muck; when planes landed, they sent up sprays of mud that obscured the vision of landing crews. During the winter the mud froze solid, and it got so cold that a man could be standing in front of a red-hot stove and still get frostbite on his back. On the ground or in the air, the Aleutian war was extremely trying.

To defeat the Japanese in the Aleutians, the United States had to employ the same maneuvers as those being used in the South Pacific. The U.S. Army Air Corps—there was no U.S. Air Force yet—would take an island, build an airfield, and then use that landing strip to take the next strategic location.

While the U.S. military could not solve the problem of the miserable weather, it did make the landing strips more functional by bringing in "Marston matting." So named because it was tested in Marston, North Carolina, each piece of matting looked like a ten-foot-long, fifteen-inch-wide piece of metal Swiss cheese. There were slots and hooks on the sides of each mat so that it could be attached to its neighbor. In this way, mat by mat, an entire landing strip could be constructed.

But it took a lot of the matting to make a runway. To cover a landing strip 5,000 feet long and 150 feet wide, it took 60,000 sheets of matting, a few dozen sledgehammers, and quite a few infantrymen with raw hands and bruised knuckles. The mats could not just be laid out on the muskeg. The earth had to be leveled, which generated quite a bit of mud.

Though the mats provided the planes with a landing surface more solid than mud, there was still more than enough mud to go around during the wet season. Whenever a plane touched down, it was usually followed by a spray of mud. Sometimes loose pieces of matting would snap free of the landing field and dance about before rolling to a stop. Other times the matting would undulate like an ocean wave under the weight of the incoming plane.

Marston matting, ten feet long by fifteen inches wide. This interlocking, Swiss cheese—like steel matting was used by the military to make landing fields during the Second World War. (Photograph courtesy of Steven C. Levi)

For many of the American pilots trained in the Lower 48, conditions in Alaska generally and in the Aleutians particularly were unexpectedly grim. While they had faith in their own fighters, they marveled that the Alaska bush planes could stay aloft. "Spare parts flying in formation," one of the Alaska bush pilots lovingly called his plane. But the Army pilots quickly grew to respect these planes, which often landed by "cracking up easy." These Alaskan planes, the Army pilot noted, "ha[d] nine lives—like a cat." But the humor aside, they respected the planes because they performed. And more than one military pilot came to feel that "the more I see the bush pilots fly, the less I fear an airplane."[17]

Even though the Japanese were only on two islands at the end of the Aleutians, Alaskans all across the Territory were on a war footing. Everyone was jumpy. Bob Reeve was almost shot down when he flew into Juneau unannounced. When asked why he had not called ahead, Reeve reportedly snapped, "I would have circled around so you could see me, but this happens to be an airplane, not a balloon, and I [was] out of gas and had to come down."[18] Even though he had a radio, Reeve rarely used it. "What do I want with a radio?" he supposedly asked the CAA. "I have enough troubles of my own without fooling with a gadget like that." You have to have a radio because it's required, he was told. So Reeve had a radio, but for months he refused to use it.[19]

On the other hand, Archie Ferguson *loved* his radio. He'd talk to anyone anytime anywhere—even when talk was restricted. One of the best-known incidents of Archie's career occurred during the Second World War when Archie was babbling into his microphone. The radio operator at Nome came on the air and told Archie that only authorized chatter was allowed on the radio except in case of emergency.

"Cessna Two Zero Seven Six Six, do you declare this an emergency?" the radio operator asked.

"Yer darn right," snapped Archie. "Anytime I'm in the air it's an emergency!"

There were still the day-to-day risks of being a bush pilot, and the close scrapes are legendary. Flying from Cold Bay in the Aleutians to Anchorage in the middle of the war, Bob Reeve encountered an ice storm and soon found that his plane was flying like a "hay barn." He had no de-icing equipment and couldn't land because it was pitch dark. So he kept flying. Eventually the icing became so bad he could not see through his windshield, so he opened the side window and navigated along the beach line of Cook Inlet. By the time he reached Anchorage he was only 200 feet off the ground and his prop was barely turning because of the ice. When he finally touched down, the CAA inspector, Burleigh Putnam, shook his head sadly and said he didn't think it would have been possible for a plane with that much ice to stay aloft. He then began lecturing Reeve on flying in ice storms. "I get your point," Reeve told Putnam, "but I didn't pick up that ice on purpose."[20]

Gradually the American forces worked their way along the Aleutians, island by island, toward Attu. Finally, the battle for the Aleutians moved from the air to the ground. On May 11, 1943, American troops hit the beaches at Attu at three points and pinched the Japanese into a valley. The fighting was fierce, with the melting muskeg a hazard to both Japanese and American soldiers. After several weeks of shelling and firing, there were only twenty-eight Japanese left alive from a contingent of 2,600.

The victory at Attu was not the end of the war in the Aleutians. The United States invaded Kiska as well, only to discover that the Japanese had evacuated their men under cloud cover. Now, with the Aleutians clear of Japanese, American bombers could use the strategic airfields of Attu to bomb the Kurile Islands and strategic targets on the Home Islands of Japan, including Tokyo. The Aleutians began the war as a strategic card in the hands of the Japanese and ended up as a critical bombing base for the Americans.

But even though Alaska was a strategic location, it seemed that only the military took Alaska's pilots seriously. The banks certainly did not. Midway through World War II, Bob Reeve was stranded in Seattle because he didn't have enough money to buy gas to fly back to Alaska. Reeve knew only one man who might help, Fowler Martin

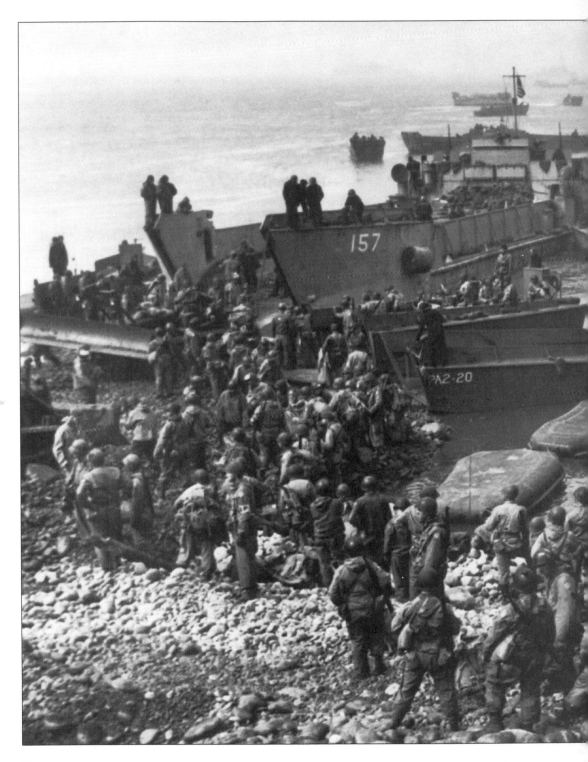

70

INVASION OF ATTU IN MAY 1943. (PHOTOGRAPH COURTESY OF THE U.S. AIR FORCE)

BOB REEVE IN VALDEZ IN THE 1930S. NOTE THAT THE REAR SKI IS HIDDEN BY THE LEFT, FRONT SKI BRACING. (WHAT APPEARS TO BE THE BRACING FOR THE REAR SKI IS ACTUALLY A PAIR OF LEGS.) (PHOTOGRAPH COURTESY OF REEVE ALEUTIAN AIRWAYS)

of the Pacific National Bank. But a loan seemed impossible: Reeve had no assets in Seattle to give the bank as security, and Pacific National Bank had a strict policy of not loaning to bush pilots. But Martin knew Reeve personally and advanced the money anyway, which did not make Martin popular with his bank. Reeve was able to repay the loan in a year, but often said, chuckling, that during that year Martin "never picked up a daily paper without scanning the headlines to see whether I had crashed."[21]

While the rest of the country was returning to peacetime activities after the war, Alaska received a sizable increase in military spending. The Pentagon had realized the area's strategic importance; with the advance of technology, Alaska became a crucial part in the defense of the United States.

7

Postwar Alaska

THE END OF THE SECOND WORLD WAR BROUGHT A technological boom to the aviation industry and an economic boom to Alaska. By the 1950s, the United States military had developed the ICBM, the intercontinental ballistic missile. During the Cold War— that time during which the United States and the Soviet Union appeared to be on the brink of a nuclear war at any moment, roughly starting in 1948 and ending in the 1980s—one of the great fears of the American military was that the Soviets would fire a missile that could reach the United States.

The U.S. military feared that it would not know when a Soviet ICBM had been fired until it was in American airspace. What they needed was more time to react so that anti-ICBM missiles could be sent aloft in time to shoot down the incoming ICBM before any damage was done.

The only way to have more time was to detect the incoming ICBMs earlier. By placing radar bases as close to the Soviet Union as possible, the military would get the maximum amount of warning time. Thus, in the mid-1950s, a string of distant early warning (DEW) sites

75

A *NORAD RADAR BASE. THE TWO "BUBBLES" CONTAIN THE ACTUAL RADAR DISHES. (PHOTO-GRAPH COURTESY OF THE U.S. AIR FORCE)*

were installed along the Alaskan coast of the Arctic Ocean. These stations would be the first to give the alarm if an incoming ICBM suddenly appeared over the horizon.

As a backup to the DEW line sites, there was a string of North American Air Defense Command (NORAD) sites as well. Also built in the 1950s, these ran throughout the Alaskan Interior and across Canada and, like the DEW line sites, were equipped with radar. If the DEW sites were knocked out, the NORAD would continue to broadcast the warning to the military bases in the Lower 48. Secondarily, the NORAD sites were to watch the skies for incoming Soviet bombers and fighters. Once Soviet planes were spotted on the radar screen, the NORAD sites would inform the American fighter aircraft at Elmendorf Air Force Base in Anchorage and Eielson Air Force Base in Fairbanks.

The oceans had to be watched as well. The Soviet Navy prowled the Bering Sea and the Soviet Air Force kept a sharp lookout for any aircraft that penetrated within 200 miles of the Soviet coast, what the USSR claimed as its territorial waters. Navigation by air was difficult because maps were only helpful near the coast. The dependable navigation system that was needed was provided by the U.S. Coast Guard in the form of LORAN, long-range navigation. A string of LORAN

U.S. COAST GUARDSMEN PLANTING TREES AT A LORAN BASE. NOTE THE LORAN TOWER IN THE BACKGROUND AND THE VEHICLES WITH TREADS FOR CROSS-COUNTRY WINTER TRAVEL. (PHOTOGRAPH COURTESY OF THE U.S. COAST GUARD)

stations stretched from southern Alaska to Port Clarence, each station broadcasting at a different frequency. Any plane with a piece of LORAN equipment would pick up the signals from three LORAN stations. Since these stations were at different points of the compass, the LORAN equipment could figure out where the plane was by the angle at which the three beams were converging. This information was then translated into terms of longitude and latitude so the pilot could pinpoint his position on a map.

But in the 1960s the LORAN equipment was so expensive that most pilots could not afford it. As a result, they flew as they always had, by the seat of their pants. This led to quite a bit of danger during polar bear hunts. Since the polar bears were found out on the ice packs, often hundreds of miles from shore, American bush pilots often strayed into Soviet airspace. In most cases the Soviets weren't that interested in the small planes flying over the ice pack, but when those planes actually landed in Siberia, they were very concerned. Then the Soviet Air Force would send their fighters aloft to harass every small plane they came across, flying so close to the small planes that the turbulence from the Soviet's jet engines would force the smaller planes down, sometimes to crash on the ice.

The U.S. Air Force also took a very dim view of the Soviets penetrating American airspace, and as soon as the incoming Soviet aircraft was picked up on American radar, American jets scrambled aloft. When American met Soviet fighter there was a courteous exchange of photos and waving. Then the Soviets were escorted back to their airspace. These confrontations between Soviet and American warplanes, known as "intercepts," were frequent. This was understandable considering that the United States claimed a 200-mile territorial limit when the distance between the Soviet Union and the United States was only a few hundred yards between the Diomede Islands and barely fifteen miles lay between the closest point of the two mainlands—with Soviet and American radar bases within eyesight of one another.

But there was still one important piece to the military puzzle missing in Alaska: communication. Because geo-stationary satellite com-

A *WHITE ALICE MICROWAVE REPEATER. NOTE THE LORAN SITE IN THE BACKGROUND. (*
TOGRAPH COURTESY OF THE U.S. AIR FORCE)

munication was still in the experimental stage, the bulk of the communication in the 1950s was done by microwave or what was known as tropospheric scatter. Combined, this system, constructed by the United States military, was known as WHITE ALICE.

Microwave did not require wires, but signals could only go between two points that were line-of-sight. In other words, microwave transmissions went in a straight line. They could not be sent over a 100-mile distance because the curvature of the earth would block the transmission. To solve this problem, huge transmission centers and smaller repeater stations were built all over Alaska. From Barrow to Ketchikan and Attu to the Canadian border, whenever an Alaskan picked up a phone, his or her voice was converted into a microwave and bounced from transmission station to repeater to repeater all across the Territory.

However, there were some parts of Alaska where it was not possible to build microwave towers or repeaters, like the Aleutians. In these areas communication beams were bounced off the troposphere from one station to the next. The troposphere, that portion of atmosphere which lies from seven to ten miles above the earth, acted much as a backboard does when a basketball is tossed against it. The radio beams, like the basketball, bounced. Sometimes these signals could be bounced as far as 200 miles.

These new technologies had a huge impact on Alaska. Every DEW, NORAD, LORAN, and WHITE ALICE station had to be built. The bulk of the building material could be shipped north by barge, but tons of it came in by plane. Carpenters and electricians were flown to the work site, and then had to be supplied with food and medicine. Mail had to be delivered. Everything from nails to a roll of toilet paper had to come by air. Before the Second World War, the bush pilots of Alaska struggled to survive on passenger service; after the war, their businesses boomed on cargo hauling. Solitary pilots formed airlines, and small airline companies, like Alaska Airlines, got much bigger.

The sudden influx of construction put money in Alaskan pockets, and the impact of those dollars was unmistakable. Alaskans could now travel more frequently, and more money went into the airlines. With more money, Alaskans bought more goods from the Lower 48, which had to be transported back to Alaska by plane. Dollars were turning over faster and the airlines were booming.

Many of Alaska's pilots also saw the end of World War II as an unexpected bonanza for aviation. As fast as the military abandoned its air bases, the pilots were there to salvage what equipment and supplies they could find. From one end of the Territory to the other, Marston matting disappeared by the mile. No sooner were the military personnel gone than pilots would swoop down on the airfields, fill their planes with the sheets of the matting, and fly them back to their local landing strip, where the matting would be reassembled. Anything that wasn't nailed down disappeared, and then reappeared on local landing strips.

Perhaps the greatest scavenger of all was Archie Ferguson. Archie wasn't satisfied with taking everything that wasn't nailed down; he went after everything whether it was nailed down or not. One summer after the war he arrived at the abandoned military airstrip of Port Clarence with his barge and proceeded to steal buildings, as many as thirty of them. He took them apart like so many modular homes, stacked them on his barge, and returned to Kotzebue. Some are still standing there today.

The old landing strips that weren't picked up are still being used, some for more than just emergencies. Those buildings that are still standing are used as shelters by hunters and downed pilots, and Alaska's bush pilots still make a living flying mail, cargo, and passengers to the NORAD and LORAN sites that are still operating. (DEW and WHITE ALICE sites no longer exist.)

For the Alaska bush pilot, World War II and the Cold War could not have come at a better time. Just when it looked as though the bush pilot was going the way of the passenger pigeon, the war gave the bush pilot a new lease on life, a lease that continues to the present day.

But new equipment could not solve all the problems. Sam Shafsky, a longtime bush pilot who flew for Archie Ferguson, remembered a flight from Ruby, up the Yukon around Tanana and then into Fairbanks in the mid-1950s. The weather had been pretty good when he started, but between Tanana and Manly Hot Springs clouds moved in, forcing him to fly lower and lower until he was skimming along inside a canyon a few hundred feet off the riverbank with mountains on each side.

"I could see something dark coming up, so I pulled over a little bit and kept looking and saying to myself, 'What the hell is that?'"

With each passing second, the object became darker. Then, in the last instant before it snapped into focus he realized it was another airplane, flying down the same canyon directly at him! The two planes were so close that neither could change course. Fortunately they were just far enough apart to whip by one another on opposite sides of the narrow canyon.

"I looked out the window and saw it was Jimmy Stewart in a Pilgrim on the mail run from Fairbanks to Nulato! I looked at him and he looked at me [as if to say] what the hell are you doing here?"

This era also highlighted many pilots of note whose experiences added to the tales of Alaska. Veteran bush pilot Tony Schultz, who spent more than forty years flying the Alaskan bush, was as famous for his willingness to fly corpses and convicts as he was for his missions of mercy. Some of his antics were legendary. In the 1950s, for instance, he was chartered by the U.S. marshal to pick up a man who was accused of killing his wife. Upon arrival in Chevak, Schultz learned that there had been a witness to the violent act who was also expecting to be flown back to Fairbanks. This made five individuals—Tony, the marshal, the husband, the witness against the husband, and the corpse of the wife—to be flown in a plane with only four seats. Schultz, a veteran at hauling cargo in the bush, was unperturbed. He put the witness on the husband's lap and then strapped both of them into a back seat with the same seat belt. After all, this was Alaska and people did things differently.

The Tourism Boom

AFTER THE WAR CAME AN EVEN GREATER BOOM: tourism. During the 1950s, Americans in the Lower 48 were suddenly flush. The G.I. Bill allowed hundreds of thousands of American soldiers to go to college. By the mid-1950s, they were reaping the rewards of a college education. These now affluent Americans were traveling, and high on their list of domestic destinations was the Land of the Midnight Sun.

Into the early 1960s, there were two traditional tours of Alaska. One was on the cruise lines following the Inside Passage along the coast of British Columbia and Alaska. This duplicated the route of Alaska's gold rush stampeders at the close of the previous century. The largest cruise line was Princess, a company still in business today. Cruises started in Vancouver, B.C., and went as far north as Skagway or Haines at the top of the Lynn Canal. This was a luxury cruise with stopovers in southeastern Alaskan cities such as Ketchikan and Juneau.

The other traditional tour began with a flight into Anchorage. From there the travelers could go south to fish for king salmon and halibut on the Kenai Peninsula. Or they could go north by train, passing through McKinley (now Denali) National Park on their way to Fairbanks. After a stay in Fairbanks, the tourists often flew back to Anchorage and then the Lower 48.

But with the boom in the tourism industry, and more and more Americans looking for the real Alaska, tour companies sprang up in communities such as Nome, Bethel, Barrow, Kotzebue, and Unalakleet. Hotels and restaurants appeared in communities that had never seen a need for such establishments. Local convention and visitors' bureaus were formed to lure tourists to exotic locations where they could see Eskimo blanket tosses, take nature tours along the Arctic Ocean, and embark upon photographic safaris on the tundra in the north or in the rain forests of the south. Small and large, the tour companies capitalized on the mystique of Alaska, its unique animals, and its stunning settings. Alaska Airlines even went so far as to paint the face of an Eskimo on the side of its planes to symbolize its roots in the northland, a feature that continues to this day.

Many of the pilots and their friends were not above making a tourism boom of their own. One October in the mid-1950s, an innkeeper in Fort Yukon by the name of Gilbert Lord devised a clever scheme to keep his hotel full during the fall. Procuring a vial of gold, he showed it to anyone who came through Fort Yukon and swore this gold had come from the bottom of a fish wheel. No one seemed to question that Lord might have an ulterior motive in wanting an influx of people in an area where he had the only hotel, and it did not take long for the word to leak out. In Fairbanks, 100 miles away, there was a general infection of the gold bug, aided by the *Fairbanks Daily News Miner* and the radio station.

All you needed was a pick, shovel, pan, and a "pack sack full of grub," remembered Fairbanks bush pilot Jim Magoffin, who was long accused of actually precipitating the "gold rush." Magoffin, a bush pilot, certainly had every reason to support it. This was, after all, probably the first stampede in world history in which the gold rushers were airlifted to the diggings. At the peak of the epidemic of gold fever, Magoffin was making four trips a day to Fort Yukon and "hardly made a dent in the line of people waiting impatiently to board our next flight."[22]

True to the spirit of gold stampedes on the Last Frontier, Bill Lavery, another bush pilot out of Fairbanks, found a more lucrative cargo. He was airlifting beer, 3,000 pounds of it on his first trip. This was 1,000 pounds over the legal load limit for his Norseman, but the profit motive was strong. His plane was so overloaded that he could not make it over the mountains to Fort Yukon, so he had to follow the Yukon River around the mountains before he could arrive at the village of Fort Yukon.

Lavery wasn't the only one trying to "get it while you can." Fairbanks merchants had set up tents all along the river in hopes of making a killing on the impending boom. But the strike only lasted about a week. When no one found any gold, the would-be stampeders, many of them suffering from acute cases of "bourbon flu," returned to Fairbanks. Then the air traffic reversed itself. That ended what was known in the Interior as the Great Fish Wheel Gold Strike.

Jim Magoffin pleaded not guilty to instigating the strike. But, as he had clearly profited from the momentary insanity, he also admitted: "I sure didn't do anything to stop it."[23]

The 1950s also brought a boom in Alaskan big-game hunting similar to the African safaris of the last century. Not only did Alaska have brown bears that tipped the scales at 1,200 pounds, there were also grizzly, moose, Dall sheep, and musk oxen. But the animal that drew hunters north, and specifically to the Arctic, was the polar bear.

Beginning in the mid-1950s and ending with the passage of the Marine Mammals Protection Act of 1972, Alaska's Arctic turned into a hunter's paradise for polar bear weighing more than half a ton and providing a skin large enough to cover a living room floor. But hunting polar bear was very dangerous. The only time to hunt the bears was when the Bering Sea had a mantle of ice three feet thick. This allowed the bears to roam on the ice pack looking for food as far south as Kotzebue.

Once ice formed on the sea, hunters boarded small planes and headed out over the ice pack. They would fly for hours, looking for

BROWN BEAR PELT. BROWN BEARS CAN GROW TO AS LARGE AS 1,600 POUNDS AND CAN RUN AS FAST AS THIRTY MILES AN HOUR. (PHOTOGRAPH COURTESY OF THE ANCHORAGE MUSEUM OF HISTORY AND ART)

86

tracks. When they saw tracks, they would follow them until they found the bear. Landing well ahead of the animal, the hunters would set up an ambush. Then, as the bear approached, they would shoot it.

Hunting this way sounds easy. It was not. The temperature averaged twenty below zero on the ice pack. If anything went wrong, like an airplane engine freezing up, the hunter and pilot might freeze to death before they could be found. It was also cold enough that guns could easily jam. Being on the ice with a jammed gun as a half-ton, meat-eating animal armed with six-inch teeth charged was not a cir-

IN THE EARLY DAYS OF ALASKA, SCENES SUCH AS THIS ONE OF A HUNTING CLUB WERE NOT UN-USUAL. (PHOTOGRAPH COURTESY OF THE ANCHORAGE MUSEUM OF HISTORY AND FINE ART)

87

cumstance many hunters favored. Polar bears had no fear of men or airplanes, which meant that if the bear was wounded and not killed, there was no telling what might happen. In the mid-1960s, Ken Oldham, a polar bear guide with a decade of seasons in the Arctic, once watched a wounded polar bear attack his *running* plane engine.

Thinking about shooting a polar bear while sitting in a comfortable room in Ohio is a bit different than actually standing behind a block of ice in temperatures ranging down to fifty below zero and watching an animal the size of a bulldozer coming straight at you. The first time Archie Ferguson went after polar bear he went with a seasoned hunter, an Eskimo by the name of Herman Ticket. They set their ambush but as soon as the bear approached, Archie lost his nerve and broke for the airplane. Clambering aboard, he started the engine and made for the sky.

Ticket, not wanting to be left alone on the ice with the polar bear, dashed after Archie. But he wasn't quick enough to make it inside the plane. The best that he could do was step on a ski. As Archie went aloft, Ticket was on the plane's ski, holding on to a strut for dear life.

In addition to all of the problems on the ice, flying conditions were especially hazardous. At that time of year the sun was only up for a few hours each day, and every pilot had to make the most of the daylight. Planes were in the air no earlier than nine A.M. and had to be back by three in the afternoon. The rest of the time it was pitch black. In addition, the ice on the surface of the Bering Sea was not flat and smooth. There were ice hills and depressions, pressure ridges and even open water stretches, called *polynyas*, as well as ice blocks as large as a house whose size could not be detected from the air. This made landing on the ice so hazardous that it did not take long for the polar bear hunters to learn to travel in pairs. One plane took the client and the second was packed to the windows with extra fuel, survival gear, and food.

The polar bear hunting era in Alaska was short. Although a polar bear is not technically a marine mammal, it was covered by the federal legislation passed in 1972. Overnight, the polar bear became a protected species. This brought to an end the polar bear trophy-hunting business in the Arctic.

The View from the Top of the World

THOUGH THE GOLDEN AGE OF THE BUSH PILOT passed with the Second World War, the Alaskan bush pilot has not vanished like the cowboy of the American West. The bush pilot still has a place in Alaska. About a third of the residents of Alaska live in the bush, and most villages do not have a runway long enough to accommodate a jet. As a result, small planes still fly passengers and cargo into and out of these communities. Whether it is a patient bound for a Fairbanks hospital, a drug counselor on her way to a conference in Anchorage, or a Native leader on his way to lobby the legislature in Juneau for a water treatment plant in his village, the trip starts in a bush plane.

But as Alaska has changed, so has the job of the bush pilot, and so have the planes and instruments. In the days of Archie Ferguson and Mudhole Smith, a compass and a radio were the only pieces of navigational equipment in the cockpit. Today, most of the bush pilots have artificial horizons, very-high-frequency omnidirectional radio range (VOR), altimeters, distance measuring equipment (DME), an automatic direction finder (ADF), gyrocompasses, and often

LORAN. Belly gas tanks extend the flying time of the aircraft, and STOL (short takeoff and landing) kits can reduce the number of feet needed for landing and takeoff on airstrips.

What this means in nuts-and-bolts terms is that a pilot can now "see" through fog and storm clouds with radar. He can pinpoint himself precisely on a map even if he is hundreds of miles from the nearest LORAN station, and can fly for hours in darkness with his plane level and his course precisely set by a distant transmission tower. He can also land without the aid of lights or flare pots. Forty years ago, this technology was nothing more than a pilot's dream.

But many of the problems faced by the bush pilots of the golden era are still present. Even with the most sophisticated weather-prediction equipment, planes and pilots still have to fly in frigid, unpredictable weather. When Alaska experienced the lowest temperatures ever recorded in the winter of 1988–89—with temperatures reaching ninety below zero in some cases—bush planes were in the air. Alaskans in remote areas were running out of supplies, and someone had to get fuel and food to them. Rugged men and women bundled themselves into parkas, bunny boots, and "fatboy" pants and flew. Day after day they flew—they were the lifeline to villages scattered across Alaska. These men and women made the difference between life and death to hundreds of Alaskans. No jet could do what these bush planes did.

In the early 1980s, Anchorage bush pilot Jim O'Meara took off from Lime Village and learned firsthand of the impact of physics on flying. It was thirty below on the runway, but once he was 3,000 feet off the ground, the temperature rose to forty degrees above zero. In a matter of minutes the temperature had jumped seventy degrees.

O'Meara appreciated the warmer temperatures, but all the way into Anchorage he kept hearing a sweeping noise on the outside of his airplane. None of his instruments gave a clue as to what the sound was, and it was only when he landed that he learned what the strange noise had been. At thirty degrees below zero, every part of his plane was at the same temperature. When he rose into the forty-above-zero belt of air, different parts of the plane warmed and expanded at

Jim O'Meara. (Photograph courtesy of Danny Daniels)

different rates. The paint on the plane expanded faster than the fuselage, so it bubbled and popped. Then the air rushing along the outer surfaces of the plane stripped the paint shreds off. By the time O'Meara landed in Anchorage, he had lost all the paint on his aircraft.

And climate conditions are still matched by human error. Today, many Alaskan bush pilots make their living flying climbers to and from Mount McKinley. Talkeetna, about seventy miles north of Anchorage, is a mecca for mountain climbers; each year, hundreds of men and women are flown up to the base camp from where they will climb to the summit.

Doug Geeting, one of the best-known mountain pilots in Talkeetna, learned a very important lesson concerning human error when he was air-dropping food around Christmas in the mid-1980s. Usually Geeting flew with a cargo handler with whom he had worked before.

For some reason he had to fly with a new cargo handler this trip, a young woman who didn't have that much experience with dropping cargo. Geeting packed his plane so he could make a number of drops. This meant stacking the cargo strategically so that as he came to the first encampment of mountain climbers, he could eject the first load of food. There was no reason to attach parachutes to the cargo because all the supplies would hit was snow, a natural cushion.

As it happened, the first encampment wanted a twenty-pound halibut. While this was a strange request for Christmas, it was no more unusual than other cargo Geeting had handled. He loaded it on board. Just before ground zero at the first encampment, he turned to his cargo handler and yelled "Halibut!"

The cargo handler, unfamiliar with her task, thought Geeting had yelled "All of it!" and so she proceeded to dump all the cargo from the back of the plane out the open hatch. A cascade of groceries

*D*OUG *G*EETING. (*PHOTOGRAPH COURTESY OF DANNY DANIELS*)

fell from the sky, hitting the camp like a bombing raid. The halibut obliterated a tent, and a case of beer smashed through another, exploding on impact and spraying the two men inside.

Feeling the plane get unusually light, Geeting turned and to his horror saw that all the goods were gone. After the cargo handler explained, Geeting turned the plane around and headed back to the encampment to assess the damage. But as soon as he approached the camp, he could see people scattering in all directions. They thought he was coming back for a second run!

Bush pilots are still called upon to make unusual rescues. In the late 1970s, Jim O'Meara was asked to rescue a climber who was stuck on a precipice near the top of a mountain. Fighting a ferocious wind, he finally made it to where the climber was marooned. The man was huddled in a tent and when he heard O'Meara he crawled out. It was his lucky day. Facing his plane into the wind, O'Meara matched his airspeed to the wind speed and then cut back on the throttle. Slowly the plane settled, coming down vertically. The plane's wheel hit the tent, and in the next instant the wind had stripped it off the mountainside. The climber reached up, grabbed the door handle, and opened the door of the settling aircraft.

93

"Once I saw his knees [and knew both his legs were in the plane]," O'Meara said, "I was gone."[24]

Sometimes the modern technology on the ground has led to improvements in flying conditions in the air. Alaskans love pizza just as much as other Americans. But some Alaskans live so far from a pizza parlor that the food has to be flown in. During the winter, many bush pilots have learned to put the sizzling pizza-to-go in plastic sacks to hold in the heat, and then place the sacks over their feet to keep them warm. "Big Mac attacks" are not unknown in Alaska; sometimes the McDonald's in Juneau receives an order for enough Big Macs to feed an entire city, which is exactly what is happening. Then bush planes take off on their "errand of mercy." There are many small communities in Alaska where McDonald's is an import.

Though modern technology has made some of the bush pilots' functions obsolete, it has opened the door to other opportunities. Through

94

BECAUSE PETROLEUM FROM PRUDHOE BAY IS HOT, THE PIPELINE IN WHICH IT TRAVELS MUST BE
INSULATED TO KEEP THE HEAT FROM DAMAGING THE PERMAFROST. ELEVATING THE PIPELINE

HELPS. NOTE THE INSULATION AROUND THE CORE OF THE PIPES. (PHOTOGRAPH COURTESY OF DANNY DANIELS)

the 1960s and 1970s, for example, televisions in Alaska picked up local stations only. All programming was done on tape delay: Programs were taped in Seattle and then flown to Anchorage and Fairbanks, where they were rebroadcast. The taped evening news came on the same day, but other programs could be a week later—or more. In some parts of Alaska it was not unusual to watch a Christmas special in February.

Cable television has made the tape delay obsolete. Alaskans can now watch football games live, enjoy CNN around the clock, or watch rock concerts on MTV. Cable television has eliminated the need for bush pilots to fly television tapes into remote communities, but it has opened the door to videotapes for consumers. The bush pilots are still carrying tapes—it's just that the tapes these days are for video stores, not television stations.

With the opening of the Pacific Rim Alaska is finding itself, once again, in a strategic geographic position. By sea, it is days closer to Japan than to Seattle, and it has two products Japan badly needs: fish and petroleum. Russia is also looking to Alaska for assistance. With the collapse of the Soviet Union, Russians in the Far East view Alaska as their cultural and economic partner. Both areas share weather, latitude, Native groups, and, most important, resources. Alaskan businesses are now operating in Siberia, and there are regular flights between Alaska and several Siberian cities. Siberian products are finding their way to the United States via Alaska, and American products are being sold in Siberia by Alaskan entrepreneurs. But both regions still have the same difficulties with weather and transportation they have always had. The Bering Sea and Arctic Ocean are free of ice for only three months each year. The rest of the year, everything needed to keep the industries operating has to be transported by plane.

The development of the petroleum industry on the shores of Prudhoe Bay on the Arctic Ocean created another boom for the Alaska bush pilot. Scientists knew there was oil in the Prudhoe Bay area, but not until the early 1970s was it economical to build the 800-mile pipeline. Today, more than a million barrels of oil a day flow from

Prudhoe Bay to Valdez, about 18 percent of the United States' daily production. Enough petroleum comes down the TransAlaska Pipeline each day to satisfy all of California's energy needs for that day.

With the development of the oil industry on the shores of the Arctic Ocean, the bush pilots had a new client. In Prudhoe Bay, where the pipeline starts, the work schedule is one week on, one week off. Men and women scheduled to work from Tuesday to Tuesday have to be flown in and out from Anchorage. Smaller planes move engineers, surveyors, and biologists all across the north slope of the Brooks Range on oil-development-related excursions. Press trips and tours by members of Congress and foreign dignitaries also have to be done in small airplanes. Security on the TransAlaska Pipeline is handled by small planes, as is the search for oil leaks and other hazards that might damage the conduit.

Small planes are also used for oil exploration and oil-spill cleanup, because only a small plane can both cover great distances and land on almost any surface. For landing on the tundra near an oil rig or an oil-slickened beach, the most inexpensive and reasonable means of transportation is still the bush plane, as long as it is flown by experienced bush pilots.

Bush planes are also used by government and private-sector biologists for wildlife population counts and transporting animals from one region to another. Archie Ferguson may have had trouble with polar bear cubs, but today live adult bears are tranquilized and flown to remote areas. The bears have not been known to wake up during the trip, but their fitful sleep has made more than one pilot nervous.

The Russian Far East also offers unlimited opportunities for the bush pilot. Like Alaska, the Russian Far East is a land of scattered, small communities and a growing petroleum industry. Pilots are going to be needed to survey the land for pipelines as well as to fly people out to hospitals and bring supplies into remote villages. The world may be changing, but in the Arctic regions, the ancient problems of weather and transportation still exist. And because of them, the Alaska bush pilot will continue to be a mainstay of the Alaskan economy and American history well into the next century.

97

Source Notes

1. Jean Potter, *The Flying North,* p. 145.
2. Fred Chambers, interview with Steven C. Levi. Levi Papers, University of Alaska, Anchorage.
3. Jim Hutchison, interview with Steven C. Levi. Levi Papers, University of Alaska, Anchorage.
4. Robert Jacobson, interview with Steven C. Levi. Levi Papers, University of Alaska, Anchorage.
5. Beth Day, *Glacier Pilot,* p. 138.
6. Day, op. cit., p. 139.
7. Ibid., p. 141.
8. Fred Goodwin, interview with Steven C. Levi. Levi Papers, University of Alaska, Anchorage.
9. Burleigh Putnam, interview with Steven C. Levi. Levi Papers, University of Alaska, Anchorage.
10. Day, op. cit., p. 136.
11. Howard Little, interview with Steven C. Levi. Levi Papers, University of Alaska, Anchorage.
12. Westover personal communication to Steven C. Levi, February 8, 1994.
13. "Munz Makes Daring Rescue," *Nome Nugget,* December 17, 1945.
14. Cordova paper, August 8, 1941. From the scrapbook of Bertha Smith, Mudhole's widow, Cordova, Alaska.

15. Cordova paper, February 19, 1940. From the scrapbook of Bertha Smith, Mudhole's widow, Cordova, Alaska.
16. Brian Garfield, *The Thousand-Mile War*, p. 135.
17. Jean Potter Chelnov, *The Flying Frontiersmen*, p. 616.
18. Day, op. cit., p. 181.
19. Potter, op. cit., p. 164.
20. Day, op. cit., p. 214.
21. Ibid., p. 180.
22. Jim Magoffin, *Triumph over Turbulence*, pp. 78–81.
23. Ibid.
24. James O'Meara, interview with Steven C. Levi. Levi Papers, University of Alaska, Anchorage.

Glossary

ADF—automatic direction finder; navigation equipment that allows a pilot to "lock on" to a radio frequency and follow the electronic beam.

Al–Can—the Alaska–Canada Highway, now known as the Alaska Highway. Built at the start of the Second World War, the highway connected Alaska with the Lower 48. Originally a dirt-and-gravel road that turned to mud in the winter, it is now paved.

"Alaskan daisy"—a fifty-five-gallon barrel. So many of these were abandoned in remote parts of Alaska that today such drums are nicknamed Alaskan daisies because, as the old saying goes, "they sprout everywhere."

Alaska Highway—the current name for the Al–Can Highway.

Aleut—a Native of the Aleutian Islands.

Aleutian Chain—the chain of islands reaching westward from the Alaskan mainland toward Siberia.

altimeter—navigation equipment that shows how high a plane is flying.

anti-ICBM missiles—missiles designed to intercept incoming intercontinental ballistic missiles (ICBMs) and destroy them in the air before the ICBMs hit their designated targets.

artificial horizon—navigation equipment that shows if a plane is flying level.

Athabaskan—Alaska's only Natives who are "Indian." The Athabaskans live in Alaska's interior. The three other Native groups in Alaska are the Eskimos, Aleuts, and Tlingit-Haida-Tsimshian.

barabara—the winter dwelling of the Eskimos of Alaska. Though it is sometimes called an igloo, the barabara is made of driftwood, sod, and sometimes whalebone. Part of the structure is belowground. Alaskan Eskimos do not live in snow-and-ice igloos.

belly tank—an auxiliary gas tank attached to the "belly" or bottom of a bush plane to give it extended range.

biplane—plane with two sets of wings. The bottom set was attached to the base of the fuselage, while the top set stretched over the cockpit. Struts secured the wing sets to each other and were sometimes used to anchor cargo that could not fit inside the craft.

bunny boots—oversized white plastic boots issued by the military that use air for insulation. They are called bunny boots because they are so oversized they look like jackrabbit feet. The boots have a valve so that when they are used in an airplane the pressure in them can be released. Bush pilots have been known to surreptitiously twist the valve of a *chee-chako*'s bunny boots closed so that when the plane rises several thousand feet, the *chee-chako*'s feet are squeezed uncomfortably.

bush—any place in Alaska that cannot be reached by a road that connects with the Lower 48. Approximately a third of Alaska's people live in the bush.

102

bush pilot—a pilot who makes his or her living flying cargo, passengers, supplies, and animals into and out of the bush.

bush plane—a plane used in the bush. Usually the term designates a plane that is unquestionably dependable. Sometimes the plane has added adaptations for use in the bush, such as STOL, belly tanks, or tundra tires.

bypass mail—a special class of mail in Alaska that allows a wider variety of items to be sent through the U.S. Postal Service. Some unusual items that are sent via bypass mail in Alaska would include tons of bricks and cinder blocks, milk cartons full of milk, steel pipes, animals in cages, snow machines, and ATVs (all-terrain vehicles).

"call and wait"—the method by which bush residents arrange for a bush plane. They *call* in their request for transportation *and wait* for a plane to arrive.

cheechako—a tenderfoot or newcomer; someone who has not spent a winter in Alaska from freeze-up to break-up. The term allegedly arose when a Skagway Native asked a newcomer where he was from. "Chicago," replied the tenderfoot. *"Cheechako,"* replied the Native, and the term stuck.

conservation—the practice of preserving natural resources and vistas for future generations.

crab—to angle a plane to take advantage of the wind. If you go to a small airport on a windy day you will see planes landing that appear to be "coming in sideways." This is crabbing. If a strong wind is blowing across the runway, a pilot will turn his plane into the wind—or "crab"—so that he can use the wind to slow his plane. On takeoff, the pilot would crab into the wind so he could increase the surface area of the wings that is exposed to the wind.

DEW—distant early warning. DEW sites are a string of radar installations on the shore of the Arctic Ocean designed to detect incoming ICBMs from what was once the Soviet Union.

DME—distance measuring equipment; navigation equipment that measures the distance between the airplane and the VOR station. (*See* **VOR.**)

Eskimos—Natives who live along the coastlines of Alaska as far south as the Bethel area.

fatboy pants—thick nylon insulated pants, originally issued by the military, which are very warm but make the wearer look grossly overweight.

flare pot—any device placed on a landing strip that will indicate the runway. In the golden age of the bush pilot, a flare pot could be as primitive as a coffee can full of diesel oil.

geo-stationary satellite—a communications satellite that orbits the earth at the same speed that the earth rotates. The satellite thus stays directly over a particular spot, and can "bounce" signals from that place to other satellites or earth stations.

gyrocompass—a compass that is not affected by the plane's motion or pitch. In other words, even if the plane is flying upside down, the gyrocompass can still be used.

103

ICBM—intercontinental ballistic missile, a missile with a nuclear warhead that had such a long range that it could be fired from well inside the borders of the U.S.S.R. and travel to the heartland of the United States.

icing—the process by which moisture in the air comes in contact with an airplane and turns to ice. For example, a pilot might be flying at 5,000 feet, where it is raining. When he drops to 3,000 feet he discovers that the temperature is below freezing. All the rain that was on his plane now turns to ice. This is very dangerous because ice adds weight to a plane.

intercepts—episodes in which fighters from the U.S. Air Force went aloft to stop Soviet airplanes from penetrating American airspace.

kuspuk—the brightly colored pullover many Eskimo women wear as an outer covering for their parka. The *kuspuk* is designed to keep the parka clean.

line of sight—Since microwave communication beams cannot bend over the horizon, they must be transmitted along a line of sight. Every transmission must be sent to a visible receiver. These receivers, called repeaters, are spaced across Alaska in straight lines.

LORAN—long-range navigation. LORAN signal centers, established by the U.S. Coast Guard, can be monitored by ships, boats, and planes to triangulate their exact position on a map. LORAN is so accurate that 1,000 miles away from the LORAN station, the LORAN machine will be within 1,000 feet of perfect accuracy.

Lower 48 — the 48 contiguous states of the United States.

Marston matting — Swiss cheese–like metal matting used as temporary landing fields. It was named Marston matting because it was first tested in Marston, North Carolina.

mukluks — Eskimo winter boots.

muktuk — whale skin and fat, an Eskimo delicacy.

muskeg — tundra in the Aleutian Islands.

NORAD — North American Air Defense Command. NORAD radar sites were established in the Alaskan interior to track incoming ICBMs and Soviet aircraft once they had been detected by the DEW sites.

oomiak — large Eskimo boat.

Outside — to an Alaskan, the Lower 48.

parka — Eskimo winter jacket.

polynyas — large, permanent stretches of open water in the ice pack. *Polynyas* are natural and can be formed by upwellings or warm-water springs beneath the surface. A *polynya* is not a "lead." A lead is a *temporary* stretch of open water, usually between two sheets of floating ice.

pontoons — large flotation devices for landing on water that many bush planes use instead of wheels.

rail belt — any place in Alaska between Seward and Fairbanks that has access to the Alaska Railroad.

RATNET — Rural Alaska Television Network, the state-owned television broadcast network. Today cable television is available in many communities.

ring of fire — the "ring" of lands and islands around the Pacific where volcanic activity is prevalent.

scramble — an episode in which U.S. Air Force planes must take off to intercept incoming Soviet aircraft.

sourdough — a seasoned Alaskan, one who has lived through a winter from freeze-up to break-up.

STOL — short takeoff and landing, STOL adaptations to bush planes make it possible for them to land on and take off from short landing strips.

taku — a strong winter wind in Southeast Alaska that blasts up the Inside Passage in gusts powerful enough to blow cars off roads.

termination dust — the first snow of winter that dusts the tops of the mountains. Its name arose because its arrival meant that many people would be terminating what they were doing, and leaving Alaska before the deep snow and cold of winter came.

Thousand-Mile War — World War II in the Aleutians, with the Japanese holding one end of the island chain and the Americans the other.

Tingmayuk — the Eskimo word for "bird," and also the name of the first plane to attempt to fly in Alaska.

Tlingit-Haida-Tsimshian — one of the four Native ethnic groups in Alaska. These three closely related peoples live in southeast Alaska.

tropospheric scatter — the practice of bouncing a communications beam off the troposphere, that belt of atmosphere seven to ten miles above the surface of the earth. It is called scatter because while a tight radio beam could be shot upward, it scattered as it bounced down and had to be collected by huge antenna, which resembled drive-in movie screens but were many times larger.

tundra — Alaskan swampland, with many mosquitoes and low vegetation.

tundra tires — large, apparently overinflated tires used by bush planes to land on the tundra.

VOR — VHF omnidirectional radio range finder, a navigational aid that can find and "lock on" to a direction beam.

wetland — *See* **tundra.**

williwaw — a sudden, violent, unpredictable wind-and-storm system prevalent in the Aleutian Islands.

Bibliography

Alaska Almanac. Seattle: Alaska Northwest Publishing Company, 1988.

Alaska's Native People. Seattle: Alaska Geographic, 1979.

Anchorage Centennial Commission, Aviation Committee. *100 Alaska Bush Pilots.* 1967.

Bits and Pieces of Alaskan History. 2 vols. Seattle Alaska Northwest Publishing Company, 1982.

Brink, Frank. *Sounds of Alaska* (record).

Bruder, Gerry. *Heroes of the Horizon.* Seattle: Alaska Northwest Books, 1991.

Bush Pilots. Editors of Time-Life Books. Alexandria, VA: Time-Life Books.

Cernick, Cliff. *Skystruck: True Tales of an Alaska Bush Pilot.* Seattle Alaska Northwest Books, 1989.

Chelnov, Jean Potter. *The Flying Frontiersmen.* New York: Macmillan, 1956.

Cloe, John Haile. *The Air Force in Alaska.* Anchorage: Office of History, Alaskan Air Command, 1986.

———. *The Aleutian Warriors.* Missoula, MT: Pictorial Histories, 1991.

Cohen, Stan. *Flying Beats Work.* Missoula, MT: Pictorial Histories, 1988.

———. *The Forgotten War* Volumes I, II, III, and IV. Missoula, MT: Pictorial Histories, 1988.

Cole, Dermot. *Frank Barr: Bush Pilot in Alaska and the Yukon.* Seattle: Alaska Northwest Publishing Company, 1986.

Cole, Terrance. "It Never Got Off the Ground," *Alaska-Yukon Magazine,* insert in *Alaska Magazine,* March 1984.

Day, Beth. *Glacier Pilot.* Sausalito, CA: Comstock, 1981.

Emmons, George Thornton. *The Tlingit Indians.* Seattle: University of Washington Press, 1991.

Fejes, Claire, *Villager.* New York: Random House, 1981.

Garfield, Brian. *The Thousand-Mile War.* New York: Bantam, 1969.

Greiner, James. *Wager with the Wind: The Don Sheldon Story.* New York: Rand McNally, 1974.

Harkey, Ira. *Pioneer Bush Pilot.* Seattle: University of Washington, 1974.

Helmricks, Harmon. *The Last of the Bush Pilots.* New York: Bantam, 1969.

Janson, Lone E. *Mudhole Smith.* Seattle: Alaska Northwest Publishing Company, 1981.

Jefford, Jack. *Winging It.* New York: Rand McNally, 1981.

Jones, Vernard E. *How I Became an Alaskan Bush Pilot.* New York: Carlton Press, 1983.

Krause, Aurel. *The Tlingit Indians.* Seattle: University of Washington, 1956.

Magoffin, Jim. *Triumph over Turbulence.* Fairbanks: Self-published, pp. 78–81.

Miller, Polly, and Leon Gordon. *Lost Heritage of Alaska.* Cleveland: World Publishing, 1967.

Mills, Stephen E. *Arctic War Birds: Alaska Aviation of World War II.* Seattle: Superior Publishing, 1971.

———. *Sourdough Sky: A Pictorial History of Flights and Flyers in the Bush.* Seattle: Superior Publishing, 1969.

Nelson, Edward William. *The Eskimo About the Bering Strait.* Washington, D.C.: Smithsonian Institution Press, 1983.

Oswalt, Wendell H. *Alaskan Eskimo.* San Francisco: Chandler Press, 1967.

Potter, Jean. *The Flying North.* New York: Macmillan, 1945: hardcover; 1947: paperback.

Satterfield, Archie. *The Alaska Airlines Story.* Seattle: Alaska Northwest Publishing Company, 1981.

———. *Alaska Bush Pilots in Float Country.* Seattle: Superior Publishing Company, 1969.

Stevens, Robert W. *Alaska's Aviation History.* Des Moines, WA: Polynyas Press, 1990.

Sturtevant, William C. *Handbook of North American Indians.* Vols. 4 and 5. Washington, D.C.: Smithsonian Institution Press, 1984.

Wilson, Jack. *Glacier Wings and Tales.* Anchorage: Great Northwest Publishing Company, 1988.

Index

111